CLASSIC
NORDIC
KNITS FOR KIDS

CLASSIC
NORDIC
KNITS FOR KIDS
21 BEAUTIFUL DESIGNS

TRINE FRANK PÅSKESEN

SEARCH PRESS

First published in the UK in 2024 by
Search Press Limited
Wellwood, North Farm Road,
Tunbridge Wells, Kent TN2 3DR

© Turbine 2017

English translation by Burravoe Translation Services

Photos: Lise Høyer Sørensen
Layout: Nanna Påskesen

ISBN: 978-1-80092-212-9
ebook ISBN: 978-1-80093-195-4

Suppliers
If you have difficulty in obtaining any of the materials and equipment mentioned in this book, then please visit the Search Press website for details of suppliers:
www.searchpress.com

Bookmarked Hub
For further ideas and inspiration, and to join our free online community,
visit www.bookmarkedhub.com

You are invited to visit the author's:
Website: knitbytrinep.com
Facebook: knitbytrinep
Instagram: @knit_by_trinep
YouTube channel: @KnitByTrineP

THANKS

First and foremost a huge thank you to my mother, as she was the one who planted the idea of writing a knitting book in my mind. Thank you to my husband for his continual support, involvement, technical assistance, constructive criticism and the many hours he spent looking after the children to make it possible to get the work finished successfully. Thank you to my two little golden nuggets for being the reason why I got knitting at all and for fantastic inspiration for new projects.

A heartfelt thank you to all my fantastic test-knitters: Christina M. T. Madsen, Emilie B. Ramsdal, Ina Y. Søndergaard, Jannie L. Brok, Lene F. Nygaard, Lone Parnas, Rikke H. Nielsen, Rikke Werther, Stine Hansen, Susann R. Gröbner, Trine E. Rødskov. Thanks for your incredibly committed (nerdy) approach to the task. Not only did you devote four months of your lives to knitting over 100 pieces, you also helped with techniques, understanding, explanations and proofreading, and I am deeply grateful.

A big thank you to all the collaborators on this book. Many of you are recent start-up companies yourselves and already had too few hours in your day. Here I particularly want to say an extra thank you to Nina from Svært Fint, who really went to great lengths to satisfy my wishes with regard to clothes, and for many inspiring conversations about being an independent start-up. Also an extra thank you to Bisgaard for providing lovely shoes for all the models.

Thank you to all the yarn companies that delivered incredible high quality yarns for the book, sometimes at lightning speed.

Thank you to my talented photographer Lise Høyer, who not only worked as photographer but also helped with contacts in the fashion industry, found locations, opened her house for photoshoots and has been a major contributor to putting together the final look of the garments. I very much appreciate the good collaboration we have enjoyed.

Thank you to my talented sister, Nanna Påskesen, who, besides supporting me throughout the entire process, was also responsible for the layout of the book. I am very proud of the book and your work, and you really succeeded in creating exactly the look I wanted. Working closely with you on such a creative project has been fantastic.

Thanks to Karen S. Lauger for the careful proofreading and checking of the patterns and the text of the original book.

A huge, heartfelt thank you to the models of all ages: Andrea, Alba, Olivia, Silke Elia, Vigga, Frida, Karla, Hjalte, Carl, Wilfred, Frederik and Tjalfe, for bringing the book and its patterns to life. Thanks for your charming, smiling approach to the job. Thanks to the amazingly patient parents who made the photoshoot day an enjoyable experience, full of laughter, chat and flexibility.

And a final thank you to all of you who have supported me on Instagram and Facebook and by buying my patterns and this book. Without you, this would have been only a dream.

CONTENTS

PREFACE

For me, creativity is challenging and full of conflicting ideas with countless solutions and possibilities. It is a process that offers opportunities to learn and grow and never comes to an end. When a pattern is finished, the process continues with further development and new ideas, inspired by what you have learned from previous experience.

With this book I want to inspire you to create, challenge your own creativity and help you to see the many possible ways of making unique garments. The designs in the book are therefore all good basic designs with lovely details to challenge both new and experienced knitters.

Many of the patterns have tips on variations, so you can experiment with different colours and looks. The designs play around with textures, lacy patterns and details that combine to create beautiful and exciting effects.

In 2016, I started the company Knit by TrineP, which gave me the opportunity to work full time as a knitwear designer. Therefore, it has been very close to my heart that this book should help to create new opportunities for others and thus give something in return. So everything you see in this book is hand-picked from various Danish designers and brands, some established longer than others. They all focus on quality, sustainability, good craftsmanship and beautiful products. Some of these products were made at home in people's own living rooms, others have been sent on their way with a handwritten card. What they all have in common is that they are backed up by very hard work, emotions, visions and dreams.

So thanks to you:
– who dreamed, dared and jumped without a safety net
– who inspire, create, produce and go your own way
– who see only possibilities, not limitations.
I hope you will find this book as inspiring as I do.

THANK YOU

Trine Påskesen

f knitbytrinep   ⊙ @knit_by_trinep

ABBREVIATIONS

alt	alternate
beg	beginning
cm	centimetre(s)
dec	decrease
DPN	double-pointed needle(s)
in	inch(es)
inc	increase
k	knit
k1tbl	knit through back loop
k1 uls	insert needle under loose strand and knit together with next stitch
kfb	knit into front and back of the stitch (increasing one stitch)
k2tog	knit two stitches together
m1l	make 1 left leaning increase
m1r	make 1 right leaning increase
p	purl
patt2tog	k2tog or p2tog as the stitches appear
p1tbl	purl through back loop
pm	place marker
p2tog	purl two stitches together
p2togtbl	purl two stitches together through the back loop
p3tog	purl three stitches together
psso	pass slipped stitch over
rep	repeat
RS	right side
skpo	slip 1 knitwise, knit 1, pass slipped stitch over
sl	slip a stitch
sl1k	slip 1 knitwise
sl1p	slip 1 purlwise
sl2, k1, psso	slip 2 knitwise, knit 1, pass slipped stitch over
sl3pwyif	slip 3 purlwise with yarn in front of work
sm	slip marker from left to right needle
st st	stocking (stockinette) stitch
st(s)	stitch(es)
WS	wrong side
wyif	with yarn in front of work
yo	yarn over needle, resulting in another stitch

TECHNIQUES

Increasing

When working raglan increases in the patterns, use the method below, unless otherwise specified in the instructions.

m1l – make one left. After the raglan marker: with the left needle pick up the loop between two stitches from the front and knit into the back of it.

m1r – make one right. Before the raglan marker: with the left needle, pick up the loop between two stitches from the back and knit into it.

German short rows

This book uses the shaping method known as German short rows. Work up to the point where you will be turning the work, turn and slip the first stitch with the yarn at the front. Wrap the yarn over to the back and pull it to produce a double stitch, so one stitch becomes two. When you come to work over this stitch again, knit or purl the double stitch together as the stitches show.

It is a good idea to mark the position of the turning stitch; it makes it easier to count and you will not miss the stitch when you continue knitting.

I-cord

An i-cord is a knitted cord that is often used for ties on hats, trousers and so on.

On 3mm (UK 11, US 2/3) double-pointed or circular needles cast on 3 stitches. Move the stitches to the other end of the needle, so the yarn is now hanging from the stitch at the back. *Pull the yarn along the back of the work to the front stitch and knit all stitches.

Repeat from *.

Work to the desired length and cast (bind) off.

Twisted cord

Another possible way of making a cord that looks different from a knitted cord is a twisted cord. Cut slightly over twice the length of yarn you will need. Tie the yarn firmly round a door handle.

Begin twisting the strand until it is tight and resistant. Sometimes it may be easier to tie the yarn round a pencil and use that to twist with. Place the yarn double and let it twist by itself. Tie a knot at each end. You can also twist together several strands of varied colours to achieve a different effect.

A GOOD START

SIZES

Children are very different in size, and you need to take this into consideration when you are knitting. The advantage of knitting these clothes yourself is that you can adjust them to suit the child. I have indicated throughout the sizes by age, according to standard measurements, so that they will fit most children. The various measurements of the finished garment are given below each size, and you may find that you want to knit a size 1 year in width and 2 years in length, if these are the measurements that suit the child best. Some of the patterns, e.g. Thor, will fit in width for a long time because of the stretchy rib and in this case, it may be a good idea to make the garment a little longer and let the child wear it turned up to begin with.

TENSION (GAUGE)

Keeping the right tension (gauge) is the key to producing an article of clothing in the correct size. The needle size indicated is always just a guideline, as how tightly or loosely people knit may vary considerably. The most important thing is not whether you use the same size needles but whether your tension (gauge) matches what is given.

To keep the right tension (gauge), the number of stitches to 10cm (4in) in width, e.g. 22 stitches to 10cm (4in), and the number of rows to 10cm (4in) in height, e.g. 33 rows to 10cm (4in), must match. If your tension (gauge) is too tight/loose compared with the tension (gauge) indicated, it will mean that the garment will be either too small or too big.

The same applies to the number of rows, where you will end up with a garment that is longer or shorter, depending on whether you have fewer or more rows to 10cm (4in) in height. This will also affect the raglan shaping, which will become either too long or too short, and the armhole may end up being the wrong size.

So, to obtain the correct tension (gauge), you will need to use a larger needle size if you have too many stitches to 10cm (4in) or a smaller needle size if you have too few stitches to 10cm (4in).

HOW TO CHECK YOUR TENSION (GAUGE)

Work a sample 15 x 15cm (6 x 6in). This means you need to cast on approx. 10 more stitches than the number given in the instructions.

Some patterns require the sample to be worked in the stitch pattern and others in stocking (stockinette) stitch. This will also be given in the instructions. The reason why it is important to work the sample in pattern is that there can often be a big difference in the tension (gauge) after the pattern has been washed and stretched out.

When working tension (gauge) samples, it is a good idea to work the outer 1.5cm (½in) on all sides in garter stitch. This will prevent the edge from curling up and make it easier to measure the tension (gauge).

When the sample is finished, wash it with a wool detergent. Rinse it gently under the tap with lukewarm water. Lay it flat to dry. When dry, steam it gently with an iron held 2cm (¾in) away from the sample.

If you have worked the sample in a lace pattern, stretch it out to dry. Do this by pinning it in place on a piece of foam rubber, such as a play surface from a children's nursery. You will then be able to measure the sample.

The reason for all this preparatory work is that the knitted fabric may change considerably during washing, depending on which yarn you used. For all the patterns in this book, the tension (gauge) given is for after washing, and as some yarns expand quite a lot in the wash, it is important to measure the tension (gauge) after washing.

YARN

It is always a good idea to go with fibres and weights matching the ones given in the pattern if you want to substitute yarn. Look at the composition of fibres, length of the different yarns used and tension (gauge) on the ball band, and find an alternate yarn using that information. Make sure you always swatch to get the right gauge, then you can be sure that your work will look as intended. There are some suggestions for yarn substitution at the end of the book – see pages 140–144. The website www.yarnsub.com can also be really helpful when it comes to finding a different yarn.

CARE

When you have completed your project, wash and block it before wearing.

Wash the garment according to the instructions on the ball band. Lay it flat on a towel to dry, and stretch it out if it is a lace pattern. Lace patterns need to be opened up so they can come into their own. Stretch it gently in the same way as for the sample, by pinning it in place as evenly as possible on a sheet of foam rubber. Yoga mats and nursery play surfaces are both good alternatives.

When the project is dry, fold it neatly and place it in the wardrobe if it is not to be worn immediately. It is not a good idea to put knitwear on a hanger, as it will stretch and make the neck opening too big and the garment too long. Wash knitwear if it has become soiled, always following the instructions for the yarn, but otherwise it will only need airing to freshen it up. If it has become creased, you can smooth it out by laying it flat and covering it with a damp towel for an hour, or steam it, holding the iron 2cm (¾in) away from the garment.

You can also cover the garment with a damp towel if the edges curl up. In this case it can sometimes be a good idea to place a book on top of it to add a little weight. This will prevent the edge from rolling up again. It is particularly effective for garter stitch edges.

LOOK BOOK

Enjoy and be inspired

Charming

page 100

Arrowhead • Quilted shorts • Thor

page 50 • page 112 • page 128

Whirlwind hat • Elinor
page 70 • page 116

Fancy collar • Everyday
page 136 • page 92

Nordic Autumn Sweater • Lightning
page 122 • page 80

Everyday • Whirlwind
page 92 • page 62

Whirlwind hat • Charming

page 70 • page 100

Arrow • Arrowhead • Sheltered

Lightning
page 80

Arrowhead
page 50

Arrowhead
page 50

Thistle
page 76

Thor
page 128

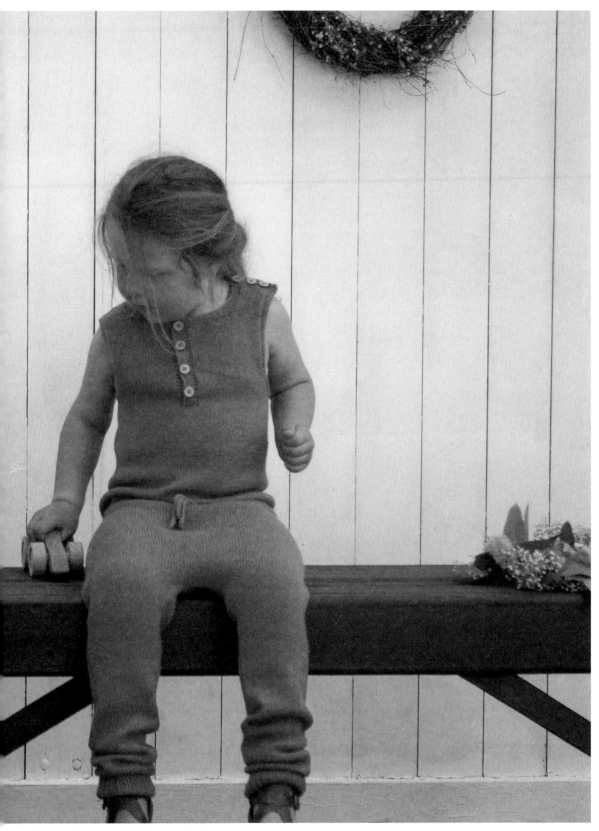

Everyday
page 92

Thistle

page 76

Nordic Autumn Sweater

page 122

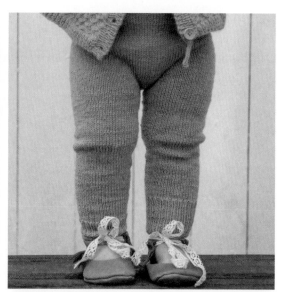

CaMaRose
Yaku 4/16

Everyday
page 92

Quilted • Sheltered
page 106 • page 132

Lightning
page 80

Charming

page 100

Charming
page 100

Quilted shorts • Whirlwind • Thor

page 112 • page 62 • page 128

Lightning
page 80

Quilted
page 106

Arrowhead • Quilted

page 50 • page 106

Arrow • Arrowhead • Sheltered
page 46 • page 50 • page 132

Quilted
page 106

Arrowhead • Quilted shorts
page 50 • page 112

Thistle
page 76

Lightning
page 80

Lightning
page 80

Whirlwind hat • Fancy collar • Elinor
page 70 • page 136 • page 116

Quilted
page 106

Quilted
page 106

Arrowhead
page 50

Fancy collar • Elinor
page 136 • page 116

Nordic Autumn Sweater

page 122

Sheltered
page 132

Everyday
page 92

Fancy collar • Everyday
page 136 • page 92

Sandnes
Alpaca Silk

Svala

page 86

Everyday
page 92

Fancy collar • Whirlwind
page 136 • page 62

ARROW

Arrow is a charming, feminine bonnet with a pretty lacy pattern. I have been crazy about this motif for ages, especially as it is both simple and complex, easy and yet challenging. The actual motif itself is built up in several layers and you start by working the arrowhead and shaft. Then you go on to the feathers of the arrow, which become more complicated as the lace pattern is worked on both right and wrong sides. The motif can be broken down to just the arrowhead, and that is how the next pattern, Arrowhead (page 50), came about.

This pattern is fun to knit and captivating as you see progress on every row. The arrowhead produces a really pretty edge and the circular finish at the neck is the icing on the cake.

Bonnets are extremely popular and especially good for keeping infants and babies warm, but of course they can also be worn by older children to add a little bit extra to any kind of outfit.

Arrow goes very well with the Arrowhead patterns. For example, you could knit a layette consisting of a bonnet and little romper for a newborn.

Sizes:
Newborn (3 mths:6 mths:9 mths:
1–2 yrs:3–4 yrs)

Measurements:
To fit head circumference:
35–40(40–42:42–44:44–46:48–52:
52–53)cm / 13¾–15¾(15¾–16½:16½–
17¼:17¼–18:19–20½:20½–20¾)in

Yarn:
1 ball of CaMaRose Yaku 4/16 (4-ply/
fingering); 50g/1¾oz /200m/219yd
Shown in Pudder (powder) (1232)

Suggested needles:
3.5mm (UK 9/10, US 4) needles;
3.5mm (UK 9/10, US 4) circular
needle, 60cm (24in) long;
3.5mm (UK 9/10, US 4) DPN
(to work i-cord)

Tension (gauge):
27 sts to 10cm (4in) in st st on 3.5mm
(UK 9/10, US 4) needles

Edge stitches:
The first and last stitches of the rows
in the first part of the work are edge
stitches and worked knitwise on
all rows

PATTERN NOTES

The bonnet is worked in rows with a lace pattern at the front.
After that it is joined to the neck and worked in rounds in stocking (stockinette) stitch. The lace pattern is shown in the chart on page 49.

HAT

On 3.5mm (UK 9/10, US 4) circular needles cast on 67(75:83:91:99:115) sts and work in rib in rows as follows:
Row 1 (WS): k1, (p1, k1) to end.
Row 2: k1, (k1, p1) to last 2 sts, k2.
Repeat last 2 rows until ribbing measures 2cm (¾in).

Next row (RS): edge st, work lace pattern from chart to last st, repeating the 8-st repeat 8(9:10:11:12:14) times, edge st.

Continue until all 30 rows of the chart have been worked.
After completing the chart work in st st until work measures 9(10:11:12:13:14)cm / 3½(4:4¼:4¾:5:5½)in from cast-on (bound-on) edge, ending on a WS row.
Next row (RS): k1, skpo, k to last 4 sts, sl1, k2tog, psso, k1.
64(72:80:88:96:112) sts.

SHAPE CROWN

Join into the round and work in st st, decreasing as follows:
Round 1: (k6, k2tog) to end of round.
8(9:10:11:12:14) sts decreased.

Round 2: knit.
Round 3: (k5, k2tog) to end of round.
8(9:10:11:12:14) sts decreased.
Round 4: knit.
Continue as set, working 1 stitch fewer between each k2tog on every alt round, until you have worked a whole round of k2tog and 16(18:20:22:24:28) sts remain.
Knit 1 round and break off the yarn. Thread the end of yarn through a needle and thread it through the remaining stitches. Pull tight to close up the hole, insert the needle in the bonnet and darn in the end on the wrong side.

NECK BORDER

With 3.5mm (UK 9/10, US 4) needles, pick up stitches all the way round the neck of the bonnet, skipping approx. every fourth stitch and making sure you have a multiple of 2 stitches.
Work in rows in k1, p1 rib until the border measures 2cm (¾in) then cast (bind) off in rib.

I-CORD

Pick up 3 sts on each side of the neck border (see also Techniques, page 11). Work until the i-cord measures 20cm (8in) or desired length.

FINISHING

Darn in all the ends.

CHART

Read the chart from right to left on right side rows and from left to right on wrong side rows.

The pattern repeat (shown in the red box) is 8 stitches that are repeated across the work, after which the last stitch (RS) or the first stitch (WS) are worked knitwise.

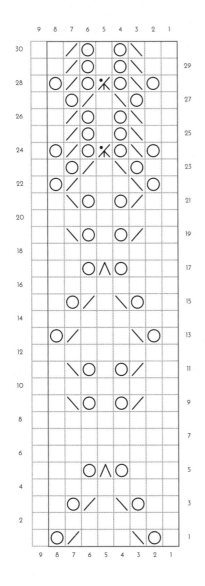

	RS: knit
□	WS: purl
O	yarn over
╱	RS: k2tog
	WS: p2tog
╲	RS: skpo
	WS: p2togtbl
∧	RS: sl1, k2tog, psso
⫟	WS: p3tog
□	pattern repeat

ARROWHEAD

Arrowhead was the first pattern I designed for the book. I had looked at the motif used for Arrow quite a lot and I thought it would be nice to have a yoke with just the tip of the motif. In order not to break up the motif, I decided to put it on a round yoke, which also finishes the neck off neatly.

The set has a simple, feminine look, not too much and not too little.

When I had knitted the yoke for the first time, I knew it had to become a set comprising a top, cardigan, tunic and romper, because Arrowhead is super for every day, very simple and easy to knit, with a nice interesting motif. The yoke is hard to put down and the large proportion of stocking (stockinette) stitch makes it a project that is easy for beginners to cope with, as well as for experienced knitters.

These garments could be part of a basic wardrobe, but the simple, pretty lace pattern also makes them perfect for a party when worn over a dress.

If you choose to make it in Yaku 4/16 wool from CaMaRose or Arwetta from Filcolana, it is perfect for everyday use – even at preschool or kindergarten – as both yarns can stand a good deal of wear and washing and still look good.

#ARROWHEAD

Sizes:
3 mths(6 mths:1 yr:2 yrs:4 yrs:6 yrs)

Top:
Chest:
47.5(54:58:64:69:73)cm /
18¾(21¼:22¾:25¼:27¼:28¾)in
Length:
25(27:31:35:38:42)cm /
9¾(10¾:12¼:13¾:15:16½)in
Buttons:
3 buttons, 13mm (½in) diameter
Yarn:
2(2:3:3:3:4) balls of CaMaRose
Yaku 4/16 (4-ply/fingering);
50g/1¾oz/200m/219yd
Shown in Lyseblå (pale blue) (1987)

Tunic:
Chest:
47.5(54:58:64:69:73)cm /
18¾(21¼:22¾:25¼:27¼:28¾)in
Length:
30:32:36:40:45:49cm /
11¾(12½:14¼:15¾:17¾:19¾)in
Buttons:
7(7:7:8:8:8) buttons, 13mm
(½in) diameter
Yarn:
2(2:2:3:3:4) balls of CaMaRose
Yaku 4/16 (4-ply/fingering);
50g/1¾oz/200m/219yd
Shown in Pudder (powder) (1232)

Romper:
Sizes:
3 mths(6 mths:1 yr:2 yrs)
Chest:
47.5(54:58:64)cm /
18¾(21¼:22¾:25¼)in

Length:
30(34:38:43)cm / 11¾(13½:15:17)in
Buttons:
3 buttons, 13mm (½in) diameter
Yarn:
2(2:2:3) balls of CaMaRose
Yaku 4/16 (4-ply/fingering);
50g/1¾oz/200m/219yd
Shown in Råhvid (natural
white) (1000)

Cardigan:
Chest:
49.5(56:60:66:71:75)cm /
19½(22:23½:26:28:29½)in
Length:
25(27:31:35:38:42)cm /
9¾(10¾:12¼:13¾:15:16½)in
Buttons:
7(7:7:8:8:8) buttons, 13mm
(½in) diameter
Yarn:
2(2:2:3:3:4) balls of Filcolana
Anina (4-ply/fingering);
50g/1¾oz/210m/230yd
Shown in Arctic Blue (1061)

Suggested needles (all patterns):
3mm (UK 11, US 2/3) circular
needles, 40–60cm (16–24in) long;
3.5mm (UK 9/10, US 4) circular
needles, 40–60cm (16–24 in) long;
3mm (UK 11, US 2/3) DPN;
3.5mm (UK 9/10, US 4) DPN.

Tension (gauge):
27 sts and 38 rows to 10cm (4in)
in st st on 3.5mm (UK 9/10,
US 4) needles

PATTERN NOTES

All the Arrowhead patterns are worked from the top down with a pretty, lace circular yoke and are worked in rows until the end of the chart. The body is then completed in stocking (stockinette) stitch, and aside from the cardigan, all patterns are then worked in rounds to the end.

The top, romper and tunic all have an opening at the back of the neck, which is fastened with buttons.

The lace pattern is shown in the chart on page 61.

TOP

YOKE

On 3mm (UK 11, US 2/3) circular needles cast on 89(89:107:107:107:107) sts.
Row 1: (WS) k4, (p1, k1) to last 5 sts, p1, k4.
Row 2: (RS) k2, yo, k2tog (buttonhole), k1, (p1, k1) to last 4 sts, k4.
Row 3: as row 1.
Row 4: k5, (p1, k1), rep to last 4 sts, k4.
Continue working rows 3 and 4 until the rib border measures 2cm (¾in), ending on a WS row.
Change to 3.5mm (UK 9/10, US 4) needles.

PLACE CHART

Row 1 (RS): k4, work chart to last 4 sts, k4.
Row 2 and all alt rows: k4, work chart to last 4 sts, k4.
Cont as set, work rows 3–4 of chart.
Row 5: k2, yo, k2tog (buttonhole), work chart to last 4 sts, k4.
Cont as set, work rows 6–14 of chart.
Row 15: as row 5.
Cont as set, work rows 16–20 of chart.

Close up the bottom of the back opening as follows:

Row 21: patt to last 4 sts. Pm to mark start of the round and transfer the last 4 sts worked to a spare needle. Join the first 4 sts of the left needle to the last 4 sts on the spare needle as follows:
Hold the 4 sts of the left needle at the front and the 4 sts on the spare needle at the back. Insert the right needle knitwise in the first stitch of the left needle, but do not slip it off the needle.

Insert the needle knitwise in the first stitch on the spare needle.
Knit the 2 sts together and slip them off the needle.

Knit the remaining 3 stitches of each needle together in the same way and place a marker.
4 sts decreased.
175(175:213:213:213:213) sts.
Continuing to work in rounds, work row 22 of chart.

Sizes 3 mths and 1 yr:
Round 23: k2, *k2, m1l, k3, m1l, k9, m1l, k3, m1l, k2*, rep from * to * to last 2 sts, k2.

Size 6 mths:
Round 23: k2, *k2, m1l, k3, m1l, k9, m1l, k3, m1l, k2*, rep from * to * to last 2 sts, k2.
Rounds 24–26: knit to end of round.
Round 27: *k7, m1l, k9, m1l, k3, m1l, k4*, rep from * to * to last 4 sts, k4.

Size 2 yrs:
Round 23: k2, *k2, m1l, k3, m1l, k9, m1l, k3, m1l, k2*, rep from * to * to last 2 sts, k2.
Rounds 24–26: knit to end of round.
Round 27: k2, *k7, m1l, k9, m1l, k7*, rep from * to * to last 2 sts k2.

Size 4 yrs:
Round 23: k2, *k2, m1l, k3, m1l, k9, m1l, k3, m1l, k2*, rep from * to * to last 2 sts, k2.
Rounds 24–26: knit to end of round.
Round 27: *k7, m1l, k9, m1l, k3, m1l, k4*, rep from * to * to last 4 sts, k4.
Rounds 28–30: knit to end of round.

Round 31: k4, *k8, m1l, k18*, rep from * to * to end of round.

Size 6 yrs:
Round 23: k2, *k2, m1l, k3, m1l, k9, m1l, k3, m1l, k2*, rep from * to * to last 2 sts, k2.
Rounds 24–26: knit to end of round.
Round 27: *k7, m1l, k9, m1l, k3, m1l, k4*, rep from * to * to last 4 sts k4.
Rounds 28–30: knit to end of round.
Round 31: k2, *k8, m1l, k9, m1l, k9*, rep from * to * to last 2 sts, k2.

All sizes:
After all the increases there are 211(238:257:279:301:312) sts on the needle.

+ If you are making the tunic or the romper, continue with the sections for these.

Cont in st st until the work measures 9(10:10:11:12:13)cm / 3½(4:4:4¼:4¾:5) in from the cast-on (bound-on) edge.

DIVIDE FOR SLEEVES
On the next round transfer the stitches for the sleeves to scrap yarn as follows:
Knit 31(35:38:42:46:48) (back 1), transfer 47(52:56:59:63:65) sts to scrap yarn (right sleeve), cast on 8(8:8:8:8:10) new sts at underarm, knit 59(68:73:81:87:90) (front), transfer 47(52:56:59:63:65) sts to scrap yarn (left sleeve), cast on 8(8:8:8:8:10) new stitches at underarm, knit 27(31:34:38:42:44) (back 2). 133(150:161:177:191:202) sts.

On the following round, knit the first and last stitches of the newly cast-on sleeve sts together with a stitch of the front or back. 129(146:157:173:187:198) sts.

BODY

Continue in st st until work measures 23(25:29:33:36:40)cm / 9(9¾:11½:13:14¼:15¾)in from cast-on (bound-on) edge.

Change to 3mm (UK 11, US 2/3) needles.

Sizes 3 mths, 1 yr, 2 yrs and 4 yrs:
Next round: k2tog, p1, (k1, p1) to last st, k1. 128(146:156:172:186:198) sts.

All sizes:

SLEEVES

Transfer the stitches for the sleeves back on to a 3.5mm (UK 9/10, US 4) circular needle and cast on 6(6:6:6:6:8) new stitches at the underarm and join to work in the round. 53(58:62:65:69:73) sts.
Place a marker for the start of the round at the centre bottom of the armhole.
Work in rounds in st st until work measures 2cm (¾in), then dec 1 st on each side of the marker.
Repeat decrease every 2cm (¾in) a further 5(6:7:8:10:12) times. 41(44:46:47:47:47) sts.

Continue without shaping until the sleeve measures 12(14:18:21:24:28) cm / 4¾(5½:7:8¼:9½:11)in.

On the last round decrease 7(8:6:7:5:3) sts, evenly spaced. 34(36:40:40:42:44) sts.

Change to 3mm (UK 11, US 2/3) needles and work 2cm (¾in) in k1, p1 rib.
Cast (bind) off in rib.

FINISHING

Darn in all the ends and sew 3 buttons on the neck opening to correspond with buttonholes.

TUNIC

Work as for the Top to +

Sizes 1 and 2 yrs:
Cont in st st until work measures 10cm (4in), measured from the neck ribbing.

All sizes:

DIVIDE FOR SLEEVES

There are 211(238:257:279:301:312) sts on the needle.
On the next round mark the stitches for the sleeves by placing markers as given below.
The sleeves are worked in k1, p1 rib. For the sizes with an uneven number of stitches, simply work an extra k1 at the end.

Round 1: k31(35:38:42:46:48) (back 1), pm, rib 47(52:56:59: 63:65) (right sleeve), pm, k59(68:73:81:87:90) (front), pm, rib 47(52:56:59:63:65) (left sleeve), pm, k27(31:34:38:42:44) (back 2).

Work st st across the back and front and (k1, p1) rib across the sleeve sts until the ribbing on the sleeves measures 2cm (¾in).

Next round: k31(35:38:42:46:48) (back 1), cast (bind) off 47(52:56:59:63:65) sts in rib (sleeve), k59(68:73:81:87:90) sts (to include last cast-(bound-)off st) (front), cast (bind) off 47(52:56:59:63:65) sts in rib (sleeve), k27(31:34:38:42:44) (to include last cast-(bound-)off st) (back 2).

Next round: *knit to cast (bind) off sts, cast on 6(6:6:6:6:8) sts, pm between the middle two new sts*, rep from * to * once more, knit to end of round.

129(146:157:173:187:198) sts.

++

BODY
Cont in st st in rounds for 2(2:2:2.5:2.5:3)cm / ¾(¾:¾:1: 1:1¼)in, ending on a WS row.

Next round (RS inc): *knit to 1 st before marker, m1r, k2, m1l*, rep from * to * once more, knit to end of round. 4 sts increased.

Increase in this way a total of 9(10:12:10:12:11) times with 2(2:2:2.5:2.5:3)cm / ¾(¾:¾:1:1:1¼in) between the increase rounds. 165(186:205:213:235:242) sts. Knit until work measures 30(32:36:40:45:49)cm / 11¾(12½:14¼:15¾:17¾:19¼)in, or 2cm (¾in) shorter than the desired overall length.

Change to 3mm (UK 11, US 2/3) needle and work as follows:

Sizes 3 mths, 1 yr, 2 yrs and 4 yrs:
Next round: k2tog, p1, rib to end of round. 164 (-:204:-212:234:-) sts.

All sizes:
Work in k1, p1 rib until ribbed border measures 2cm (¾in). Cast (bind) off in rib.

FINISHING
Darn in all the ends and sew 3 buttons on the neck edge.

ROMPER
Work as for the Tunic to ++

Cont in st st in rounds for 3cm (1¼in), ending on a WS row.

Next round (RS inc): *knit to 1 st before marker, m1r, k2, m1l*, rep from * to * once more, knit to end of round. 4 sts increased.

Increase in this way a total of 5(5:6:6) times with 3cm (1¼in) between the inc rounds. 149(166:181:197) sts.

Cont in st st until work measures
16(17:19.5:20)cm / 6¼(6¾:7:7¾)in.

DIVIDE FRONT AND BACK

Next round: k39(43:47:51), transfer
the next 75(84:91:99) sts to a spare
needle (front).
Now complete the front and
back separately.

BACK

The back is worked in rows in st st
over the remaining 74(82:90:98) sts.
Turn the work and work back
along the row as follows:
Cast (bind) off 3 sts, work past the
start of the round to where the sts
of the front start.
Turn, cast (bind) off 3 sts and work
back along the row.
Continue in this way, casting
off 3 sts on each row, until you
have worked 20(22:24:26) rows.
14(16:18:20) sts.

Change to 3mm (UK 11,
US 2/3) needles.

Next row: k2tog, p1, (k1, p1) to last
st, k1. 13(15:17:19) sts.
Work in rib until ribbing measures
2cm (¾in).

Cast (bind) off in rib.

FRONT

The front is worked in rows in st st
over the 75(84:91:99) sts from the
spare needle.

Join the yarn on the RS and cast
(bind) off the first 4 sts, knit
71(80:87:95). Turn, cast (bind) off
4 sts and knit to end.
Continue in this way, casting off
4 sts at the start of each row, until
you have worked 10(12:12:12) rows.
35(36:43:51) sts.
Now cast (bind) off 3 sts at the start
of each row for a total of 6(6:8:8)
rows. 17(18:19:27) sts.

Size 3 mths:
Cast (bind) off 2 sts at the start of
the next 2 rows. 13(-:-:-) sts.
Change to 3mm (UK 11,
US 2/3) needles.

Size 6 mths:
Change to 3mm (UK 11,
US 2/3) needles.
Next row: k2tog, p1, (k1, p1) to
last st, k1.

Size 1 yr:
Cast (bind) off 1 st at the start of
the next 2 rows. -(-:17:-) sts.
Change to 3mm (UK 11,
US 2/3) needles.

Size 2 yrs:
Cast (bind) off 2 sts at the start of
the next 2 rows -(-:-:23) sts.
Change to 3mm (UK 11,
US 2/3) needles.

All sizes:
Next row: (k1, p1) to last st, k1.
Work until ribbing measures 2cm
(¾in), but after 1cm (⅜in) rib make
a buttonhole in the middle of the
border by working: k2tog, yo.
Cast (bind) off in rib.

LEG BORDER

With RS facing, on 3mm (UK 11, US 2/3) needles, pick up and knit approx. 79(81:83:85) sts around the leg opening.

Row 1: (k1 tbl, p1) to last st, k1 tbl. (This will reduce the size of the little holes that may occur when picking up the stitches.)
Work 1cm (⅜in) in rows in k1, p1 rib. Make a buttonhole in line with the buttonhole of the front.
Work until the ribbed border measures 2cm (¾in).
Cast (bind) off in rib. Make the second side in the same way.

FINISHING

Darn in all the ends; sew 3 buttons on the neck opening and 3 buttons on the lower fastening.

CARDIGAN
EDGE STITCHES

The first and last stitches of the rows in the first part of the work are edge stitches and worked knitwise on all rows.

With 3mm (UK 11, US 2/3) needles, cast on 83(83:101:101:101:101) sts and work in rib as follows:
Row 1 (WS): edge st, (k1, p1) to last 2 sts, k1, edge st.
Cont in rib until work measures 2cm (¾in), ending on a WS row.

Change to 3.5mm (UK 9/10, US 4) needles.

PLACE CHART

Row 1 (RS): edge st, work chart to last stitch, edge st.
Continue working the first and last sts of every row as edge sts and working the other sts in pattern following the chart until all 22 rows have been worked.

There are 173(173:211:211:211) sts on the needles after working the chart.

Sizes 3 mths and 1 yr:
Row 23: edge st, *k2, m1, k3, m1, k9, m1, k3, m1, k2*, rep from * to * to last st, edge st.

Size 6 mths:
Row 23: edge st, *k2, m1, k3, m1, k9, m1, k3, m1, k2*, rep from * to * to last st, edge st.
Rows 24–26: knit.
Row 27: edge st, *k7, m1, k9, m1, k3, m1, k4*, rep from * to * to last st, edge st.

Size 2 yrs:
Row 23: edge st, *k2, m1, k3, m1, k9, m1, k3, m1, k2*, rep from * to * to last st, edge st.
Rows 24–26: knit.
Row 27: edge st, *k7, m1, k9, m1, k7*, rep from * to * to last st, edge st.

Size 4 yrs:
Row 23: edge st, *k2, m1, k3, m1, k9, m1, k3, m1, k2*, rep from * to * to last st, edge st.
Rows 24–26: knit.
Row 27: edge st, *k7, m1, k9, m1, k3, m1, k4*, rep from * to * to last st, edge st.

Rows 28–30: knit.
Row 31: edge st, *k8, m1l, k18*, rep from * to * to last st, edge st.

Size 6 yrs:
Row 23: edge st, *k2, m1l, k3, m1l, k9, m1l, k3, m1l, k2*, rep from * to * to last st, edge st.
Rows 24–26: knit.
Row 27: edge st, *k7, m1l, k9, m1l, k3, m1l, k4*, rep from * to * to last st, edge st.
Rows 28–30: knit.
Row 31: edge st, *k8, m1l, k9, m1l, k9*, rep from * to * to last st, edge st.

All sizes:
209(236:255:277:299:310) sts.

DIVIDE FOR SLEEVES
Next row (RS): edge st, k28(32:35:39:42:44) (front 1), transfer 47(52:56:59:63:65) sts to scrap yarn (sleeve), cast on 8(8:8:8:8:10) new sts at underarm, k57(66:71:79:87:90) (back), transfer 47(52:56:59:63:65) sts to scrap yarn (sleeve), cast on 8(8:8:8:8:10) new sts at underarm, k 28(32:35:39: 42:44) (front 2), edge st.

On the next row work the first and last sts of the newly cast-on sleeve together with a stitch of the front or back. 127(144:155:171:185:196) sts.

BODY
Maintaining edge sts, work in st st until work measures 23(25:29:33:36:40)cm / 9(9¾:11½:13:14¼:15¾)in

or 2cm (¾in) from the desired overall length.

Change to 3mm (UK 11, US 2/3) needles.

Sizes 6 mths and 6 yrs:
Next row: k2tog, p1, (k1, p1) to last st, k1.

All sizes:
Work in rib until rib border measures 2cm (¾in).
Cast (bind) off in rib.

SLEEVES
Transfer the stitches for the sleeves back on to a 3.5mm (UK 9/10, US 4) circular needle and cast on 6(6:6:6:6:8) new stitches at the underarm and join to work in the round.
Place a marker for the start of the round at the centre bottom of the armhole. 53(58:62:65:69:73) sts.

Work in rounds in st st until work measures 2cm (¾in), then dec 1 st on each side of the marker.
Repeat decrease every 2cm (¾in) a further 5(6:7:8:10:12) times. 41(44:46:47:47:47) sts.
Continue without shaping until the sleeve measures 12(14:18:21: 24:28)cm / 4¾(5½:7:8¼:9½:11)in.
On the last round decrease 7(8:6:7:5:3) sts, evenly spaced. 34(36:40:40:42:44) sts.

Change to 3mm (UK 11, US 2/3) needles and work 2cm (¾in) in k1, p1 rib.
Cast (bind) off in rib.

BUTTON BAND

With RS facing and 3mm (UK 11, US 2/3) circular needles, pick up approx. 3 sts for every 4 rows along the left front edge, making sure you have an uneven number of stitches.
Next row (WS): (p1, k1) to last st, p1.
Cont in rib as the sts present until the band measures 2cm (¾in).
Cast (bind) off in rib.

Mark placement for 7(7:7:8:8:8) buttons, the first one at the centre of the neck ribbing, the bottom one at the centre of the bottom ribbing and the remainder evenly spaced in between.

BUTTONHOLE BAND

Work in the same way as the button band along the right front, but after working 1cm (⅜in) in rib make 7(7:7:8:8:8) buttonholes to correspond with markers. Make the buttonholes by casting off 2 sts on the right side row and casting on 2 new sts above these on the next row.
Continue working in rib until the border measures 2cm (¾in) and cast (bind) off in rib.

FINISHING
Darn in all the ends and sew on the buttons.

CHART

Work the chart from right to left on right side of work and left to right on wrong side rows. Rep the chart 9(9:11:11:11:11) times in a row/round and once vertically.

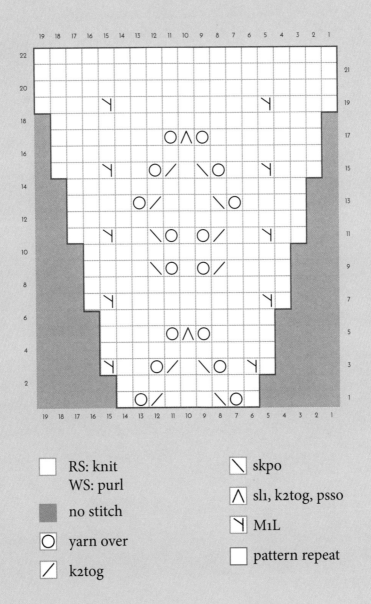

	RS: knit WS: purl		＼	skpo
	no stitch		∧	sl1, k2tog, psso
O	yarn over		Υ	M1L
／	k2tog			pattern repeat

WHIRLWIND

The inspiration for Whirlwind comes from a Japanese stitch pattern book. I fell headlong for the pretty motif used in this pattern. The structure of the motif and the way it is staggered reminds me of a whirlwind that starts off in a mad rush before calming down and then starts up again somewhere else – a bit chaotic but nevertheless very structured. As this pattern is intended to suit children aged 1–6 years who are very active, it just had to be called Whirlwind.

With this pattern I wanted to make a cardigan with a lace pattern that can be worn by both girls and boys as a cardigan or a jacket, depending on which yarn it is made in.

Lacy patterns are often very feminine and it can be difficult to find good patterns of this kind for boys. This one has a touch of masculinity to it. I have used it over the entire cardigan to enhance this look and illustrated it in various yarns, each of which produces a different effect. If you want to have a bulkier, more masculine jacket, it would be a good idea to make it in a very stretchy yarn, such as Sandnes Merinoull. If you would rather tone down the pattern so it lies flatter and hangs more lightly, say for a cardigan, you can make it in Sterk from Du Store Alpakka. This means you can decide for yourself whether you want to make a sturdy everyday jacket or a lovely cardigan that can be worn with a pretty dress for a party. Both yarns come in a great range of colours and, once again, you can enhance the effect by using mute colours to tone down the pattern or bright colours to bring it out.

The pattern is interesting to work, but still easy to get your head around once you get started.

#WHIRLWIND JACKET

Sizes:
12 mths (18–24 mths:3–4 yrs:5–6 yrs)

Measurements:
Chest:
57(63:69:75)cm /
22½(24¾:27¼:29½)in
Length:
33(37:39:43)cm / 13(14½:15¾:17)in
(measured from back neck down)

Yarn:
3(5:6:8) balls of Du Store Alpakka
Sterk (DK/8-ply/light worsted);
50g/1¾oz/137m/150yd
Shown in Lys blå (light blue) (848);
(see pages 62 and 68)
OR
4(7:8:10) balls of Sandnes Merinoull
(DK/8-ply/light worsted);
50g/1¾oz/105m/115yd
Shown in Mosegrønn (moss green)
(9644) (see page 65)

Other materials:
6(8:9:10) buttons, 15mm
(⅝in) diameter
4 stitch markers

Suggested needles:
3.5mm (UK 9/10, US 4) and 3mm
(UK 11, US 2/3) circular needles,
40–60cm (16–24in) long;
3.5mm (UK 9/10, US 4) and 3mm
(UK 11, US 2/3) DPN

Tension (gauge):
26 sts to 10cm (4in) in chart pattern
on 3.5mm (UK 9/10, US 4) needles
22 sts and 30 rows to 10cm (4in)
in st st on 3.5mm (UK 9/10,
US 4) needles

Edge stitches:
The first and last stitches of the
row are edge stitches and worked
knitwise on all rows

PATTERN NOTES

The cardigan is knitted in rows from the bottom up. The yoke is shaped with raglan decreases. There is a pretty lacy pattern on the body, whereas the sleeves are worked in stocking (stockinette) stitch.

The pattern is worked from the chart on page 69. The first and last stitches of the rows are edge stitches and worked knitwise on all rows.

BODY

On 3mm (UK 11, US 2/3) needles, cast on 144(160:176:192) sts and work in rib as follows:

Row 1 (WS): edge st, *p2, k2*, repeat from * to * to last 3 sts, p2, k1 (edge st).

Continue to work in rib as the stitches appear (working edge stitches as k1 on every row) until ribbing measures 3cm (1¼in), ending on a RS row.

Next row (WS): kfb, rib to last st, kfb. 146(162:178:194) sts.

Change to 3.5mm (UK 9/10, US 4) needles.

Next row (RS): edge st, work chart to last stitch, edge st.

Continue in pattern as set, following the chart until the work measures 21(23:24:27)cm / 8¼(9:9½:10¾)in from cast-on (bound-on) edge, ending on a RS row.

SHAPE ARMHOLES

Next row (RS): edge st, patt 32:36:40:44 sts, cast (bind) off 8 sts, work until there are 64(72:80:88) sts on the needle after cast (bind) off, cast (bind) off 8 sts, patt 32(36:40:44) sts, edge st.

Set work aside and make sleeves.

SLEEVES

On 3mm (UK 11, US 2/3) needles, cast on 36(36:40:40) sts and join to work in the round. Pm to mark beg of round. Work 2cm (¾in) in rounds in k2, p2 rib. Place a marker at the start of the round.

Change to 3.5mm (UK 9/10, US 4) needles.

Beg with a RS row, work in st st until work measures 3cm (1¼in), ending with a WS row.

Inc row (RS): k1, m1l, knit to last stitch, m1r, k1. 2 sts increased.

Increase in this way a total of 4(5:4:7) times working 3cm (1¼in) in st st between increase rounds. 8(10:8:14) sts increased. 44(46:48:54) sts.

Continue in st st until work measures 22(26:30:34)cm / (8¾:10¼:11¾:13½)in from cast-on (bound-on) edge, ending on a WS row.

Cast (bind) off 4 sts, knit to last 3 sts, cast (bind) off 3 sts and fasten off final st. 36(38:40:46) sts.

Transfer the sts of the first sleeve to scrap yarn and make another sleeve in the same way.

JOIN BODY AND SLEEVES

Insert the sleeves over the cast-(bound-)off sts of the body. Place a marker everywhere the edges of body and sleeve meet to mark raglans. 202(222:242:270) sts. Decrease on each side of the markers on every right side row as follows:

Dec row (RS): edge st, *patt to 3 sts before marker, skpo, k2, k2tog*, work from * to * a total of 4 times, knit to last stitch, edge st. 8 sts decreased.

Work one WS row, continuing to work in st st for the sleeves and in chart pattern on the body. Decrease at the raglan a total of 15(17:18:21) times, ending on a WS row. 82(86:98:102) sts.

Change to 3mm (UK 11, US 2/3) needles.

Sizes 12 mths and 18–24 mths:
Next row (RS): edge st, k1, work p2, k2 rib to last 4 sts, p2, k1, edge st.

Size 3–4 yrs:
Next row (RS): edge st, k1, k2tog (p2, k2) to last 6 sts, p2, k2tog, k1, edge st. 96 sts.

Size 5–6 yrs:
Next row (RS): edge st, work k2, p2 rib to last 3 sts, k2, edge st, at the same time decreasing to 96 sts by working (k1, k2tog) 6 times evenly in place of k2.

All sizes:
Work in 2x2 rib until ribbing measures 2cm (¾in) and cast (bind) off in rib.

BUTTON BAND

With RS facing and 3mm (UK 11, US 2/3) circular needles, pick up approx. 3 sts for every 4 rows along the left front edge to a total multiple of 4 sts plus 2 sts.
Next row (RS): (k2, p2) to last 2 sts, k2.
Continue in rib as sts appear until the band measures 2cm (¾in).

Mark placement for 6(8:9:10) buttons, the first one 1cm (⅜in) from the neck edge, and the bottom one 1cm (⅜in) from the cast-on (bound-on) edge, with the remainder evenly spaced in between.

BUTTONHOLE BAND

Work in the same way as the button band along the right front, but after working 1cm (⅜in) in rib make 6(8:9:10) buttonholes to correspond with markers. Make buttonholes by working k2tog, yo in place of k2 in the rib.

FINISHING

Darn in all the ends and sew up the underarm seams. Sew on buttons on left button band to correspond with buttonholes.

CHART

Read the chart from the bottom up, from right to left on right side rows and left to right on wrong side rows.

IMPORTANT NOTE: The first stitch on rows 13, 17 and 21 should be worked k1 instead of yarn over on the first rep only, and the last stitches should be worked as k2tog instead of k3tog on the first rep only. This is to maintain the correct number of stitches.

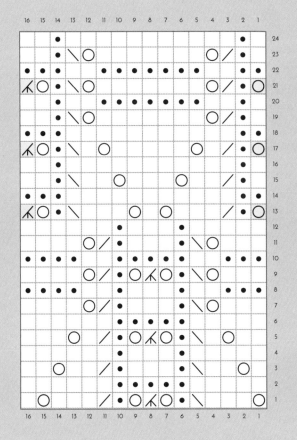

	RS: knit WS: purl
•	RS: purl WS: knit
O	yarn over
/	k2tog
\	skpo
⋏	k3tog
⋏	k2tog on first rep only, k3tog on subsequent reps
O	k1 on first rep only, yo on subsequent reps
	pattern repeat

WHIRLWIND HAT

Everyone at home is crazy about hats. The children love having several to choose from and they are delightfully quick to knit, so I just had to have a couple of hats in this book. I wanted Whirlwind to have a nice shape, fitting closely around the ears, and it also had to be interesting to knit. When I had created the stitch pattern for the Whirlwind jacket, I knew that that was what I had to use for the hat as well. I love the slightly chaotic impression produced by the lacy pattern and it is also very good fun to knit.

The hat can be worn by both boys and girls. Like the Whirlwind jacket, the pattern can be bulkier, or less so, depending on the yarn you choose. Decorate the hat with a homemade pompom or bobble to give it a little extra something.

Sizes:
6–18 mths(18 mths–4 yrs:5–6 yrs)

Measurements:
To fit head circumference:
35–41(41–50:51–55)cm /
13¼–16¼(16¼–19¾:20–21¾)in
Height (without bobble):
16cm (6¼in)

Yarn:
2(2:2) balls of Sandnes Merinoull
(DK/8-ply/light worsted);
50g/1¾oz/105m/115yd
Shown in Grå lavender (grey
lavender) (discontinued)

Suggested needles:
3.5mm (UK 9/10, US 4) DPN or
circular needles, 40cm (16in) long
using the magic loop method
3mm (UK 11, US 2/3) DPN or
circular needles, 40cm (16in) long
using the magic loop method

Other materials:
A tassel or pompom for the top of
the hat (optional)

Tension (gauge):
26 sts and 48 rows to 10cm (4in) in
chart pattern on 3.5mm (UK 9/10,
US 4) needles

PATTERN NOTES

The hat is worked in rounds from the bottom up.
Instructions are written for a version with earflaps or with a ribbed cuff.
The main part of the hat is worked in pattern.
Instructions for the earflaps are given for the two smallest sizes.
The lace pattern is shown in the chart on page 75.

Edge stitches:
The first and last stitches of the rows on the earflaps are edge stitches and are
worked knitwise on all rows

HAT WITH EARFLAPS

On 3mm (UK 11, US 2/3) needle(s) cast on 3 sts and make an i-cord (see
Techniques, page 11). Work until the i-cord measures 15cm (6in) or the
desired length. Then work as follows:
Row 1: (WS) p3.
Row 2: (RS) k1, m1r, k1, m1l, k1.
Row 3: k1 (edge st), p3, k1 (edge st).
Row 4: edge st, m1r, k1, p1, k1, m1l, edge st.
Row 5: edge st, k1, p1, k1, p1, k1, edge st.
Row 6: edge st, m1r, p1, k1, p1, k1, p1, m1l, edge st.

Continue in this way working increases and rib on every alt row plus an edge
stitch at each side of the work.
The new sts should be worked into rib as the sts appear. When there are
27 sts on the needle, including the edge stitches, finish with a WS row. Set the
work aside and make a second earflap.

SET UP HAT TO WORK IN THE ROUND
Using a 3mm (UK 11, US 2/3) needle, with RS facing, work the earflaps into
position on the same needle as follows:

Size 6–18 mths:
Rib across the first earflap as the stitches appear (27 sts), cast on 27 new
sts (forehead), rib across the second earflap as the stitches appear (27 sts),
cast on 15 new sts (back neck). Join into the round and pm to mark start of
round. There are now 96 sts on the needle. Work in 1x1 rib in rounds until
the border measures 3cm (1¼in) from the newly cast-on stitches.
Continue as shown in the chart.

Size 18 mths–4 yrs:
Cast on 12 sts (back neck 1), rib across the first earflap as the stitches show (27 sts), cast on 35 new sts (forehead), rib across the second earflap as the stitches show (27 sts), cast on 11 new sts (back neck 2). Join into the round and pm to mark start of round. There are now 112 sts on the needle. Work in 1x1 rib in rounds in rib until the border measures 3cm (1¼in) from the newly cast-on stitches.
Continue as shown in the chart.

HAT WITHOUT EARFLAPS
On 3mm (UK 11, US 2/3) needles cast on 96(112:128) sts and join to work in the round. Pm to mark start of round. Work in rounds in k1, p1 rib until work measures 5cm (2in).
Continue as shown in the chart.

SHAPE CROWN (BOTH VERSIONS)
Decrease for the top of the hat as follows:
Round 1: *k1, p1, k2tog, k7, skpo, p1, k2*, repeat from * to * to end of round. 84(98:112) sts.
Round 2: slip (move start of round), *p1, k2tog, k5, skpo, p1, sl1k, k2tog, psso*, repeat from * to * to end of round. 60(70:80) sts.
Round 3: *p1, k2tog, k3, skpo, p1, k1*, repeat from * to * to end of round. 48(56:64) sts.
Round 4: *p1, k2tog, k1, skpo, p1, k1*, repeat from * to * to end of round. 36(42:48) sts.
Round 5: *p1, sl1k, k2tog, psso, p1, k1*, repeat from * to * to end of round. 24(28:32) sts.
Round 6: *p1, k1*, repeat from * to * to end of round.
Round 7: *k2tog*, repeat from * to * to end of round.12(14:16) sts.
Break off the yarn, thread it through rem sts and pull tight.

FINISHING
Darn in all the ends on the wrong side and, if desired, sew a pompom or bobble on the top of the hat.

CHART

NOTE: On rounds 13, 17 and 21 of chart move the start of the round as follows: Remove start of round marker, slip first stitch purlwise, replace marker and then work the chart. This means the first stitch will become the last stitch of the round.

Change to 3.5mm (UK 9/10, US 4) needles and work the lace pattern from the chart as follows:

Read all chart rounds from right to left. Repeat the 16 st chart 6(7:8) times across the round and work rows 1–24 twice.

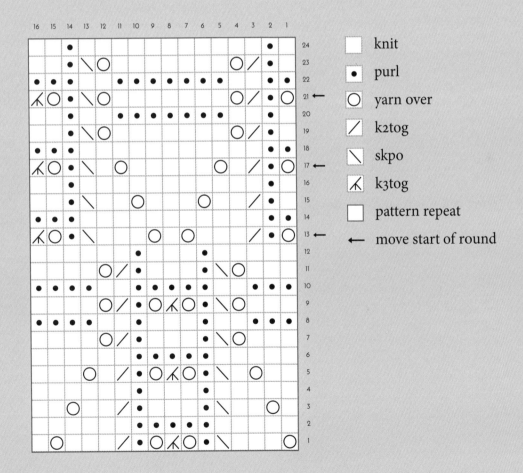

knit	
•	purl
○	yarn over
/	k2tog
\	skpo
⋏	k3tog
	pattern repeat
←	move start of round

THISTLE

The idea behind Thistle was to make a simple classic skirt that would look elegant but have an overskirt with a playful swing, so that the skirt could be worn on special occasions.

Thistle became exactly that – a simple, feminine skirt with a pretty, lacy peplum at the top. The pattern itself is quick to knit in stocking (stockinette) stitch on a 4mm (UK 8, US 6) circular needle. The peplum gives the plain skirt an extra something and provides the knitter with a little challenge. The pattern is not difficult, but as there are parts where the lace is worked on every row, it requires some concentration.

Thistle also plays about with different yarn weights. The peplum is knitted with a single strand of yarn to produce a lacy effect while the skirt uses the yarn held double to give it a sturdy look and make it more hardwearing. The pattern was named Thistle because the pretty lace effect looks a little like thistle flowers.

Sizes:
1 yr(2 yrs:3–4 yrs:5–6 yrs)

Measurements:
Hip (circumference):
50(56:59:63)cm / 19¾(22:23¼:24¾)in
Total length:
20(21:22:24)cm / 7¾(8¼:8¾:9½)in

Yarn:
3(3:3:4) balls of Filcolana Arwetta
Classic (4-ply/fingering);
50g/1¾oz/210m/230yd
Shown in Knækket hvid
(broken white) (101)

Other materials:
2.5cm (1in) wide elastic, approx
53(57.5:58:62)cm /
21(22½:22¾:24½)in long

Suggested needles:
3.5mm (UK 9/10, US 4) and 4mm
(UK 8, US 6) circular needles,
40–60cm (16–24in) long

Tension (gauge):
22 sts to 10cm (4in) in st st with
yarn held double on 4mm (UK 8,
US 6) needles.

Tip:
You can also make the skirt without the peplum, which will give you a simple, quickly made skirt for everyday wear.

PATTERN NOTES

The skirt is worked in rounds from the bottom up in stocking (stockinette) stitch with yarn held double.

The peplum is worked in rounds from the bottom up with a single strand of yarn and joined to the skirt by knitting the stitches together.

The lace pattern for the peplum is shown in the chart on page 79.

SKIRT

With 3.5mm (UK 9/10, US 4) needles and yarn held double, cast on 110(124:130:140) sts and join to work in the round. Pm to mark beg of round.

Work 3cm (1¼in) in rounds in st st then purl 1 round (fold edge).

Change to 4mm (UK 8, US 6) needles and continue in rounds in st st until work measures 20(20.5:20:22)cm / 7¾(8:7¾:8¾)in measured from the fold edge.

Size 2 yrs:
Round 1: k28, skpo, k2, k2tog, k56, skpo, k2, k2tog, k28. 120 sts.

Size 3-4 yrs:
Round 1: k30, skpo, pm, k1, k2tog, k60, skpo, pm, k1, k2tog, k30. 126 sts.
Round 2: knit.
Round 3: k29, skpo, sm, k1, k2tog, k58, skpo, sm, k1, k2tog, k29. 122 sts.
Round 4: knit.

Round 5: (remove markers as you come to them) k28, skpo, sm, k1, k60, sm, k1, k2tog, k28. 120 sts.
Round 6: knit.

Size 5-6 yrs:
Round 1: k32, skpo, k1, pm, k1, k2tog, k64, skpo, k1, pm, k1, k2tog, k32. 136 sts.
Round 2: knit.
Round 3: k31, skpo, k1, sm, k1, k2tog, k62, skpo, k1, sm, k1, k2tog, k31. 132 sts.
Round 4: knit.
Round 5: (remove markers as you come to them) k32, k2tog, k64, k2tog, k32. 130 sts.
Round 6: knit.

All sizes:
Set the work aside and make the peplum.

PEPLUM

With 3.5mm (UK 9/10, US 4) needles, cast on 220(240:240:260) sts using a single strand of yarn and join to work in the round. Pm to mark beg of round.

Work in rounds following the chart, working the 10-st pattern repeat 22(24:24:26) times across the round. Work rounds 1–16 of the lace pattern from the chart twice.
Next round (RS): (k2tog) to end of round. 110(120:120:130) sts.

JOIN SKIRT AND PEPLUM
Join the lace peplum to the skirt: Place the peplum over the skirt

so that the stitches line up, with the overskirt on the outside and the right sides of both pieces facing out. With 3.5mm (UK 9/10, US 4) needles and yarn held double, knit one stitch of the peplum together with one stitch of the skirt. Continue in this way, knitting the stitches of the peplum together with the corresponding stitches of the skirt to the end of the round.

Work 3cm (1¼in) in st st, purl 1 round, then work another 3cm (1¼in) st st. Cast (bind) off loosely.

FINISHING

Fold over the bottom edge of the skirt and sew in place on the wrong side. Fold over at the waist, threading the elastic through before sewing the edge in place.

Darn in all the ends and wash the skirt according to the instructions for the yarn.

Dry the skirt flat and block the lace peplum.

CHART

Read all rows of the chart from right to left on the right side, as you are working in rounds.

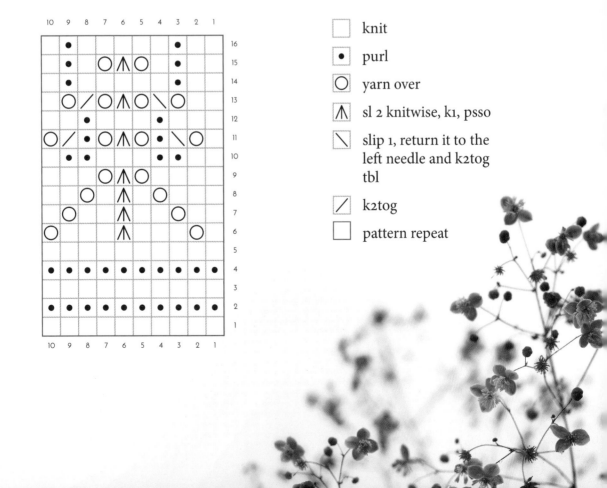

- ☐ knit
- • purl
- ○ yarn over
- ⋀ sl 2 knitwise, k1, psso
- ⟍ slip 1, return it to the left needle and k2tog tbl
- ⟋ k2tog
- ☐ pattern repeat

LIGHTNING

Lightning is a lovely, easy unisex sweater. The pattern consists only of knit and purl sts, which makes the sweater a great project for anyone who has not yet knitted many garments and would like to try something with a textured surface.

The mixture of stitches creates a nice structure that looks rather like small lightning flashes, which is how this simple sweater got its name. Lightning is perfectly suited for wearing in winter or over a nice shirt.

Sizes:
6 mths(1 yr:2 yrs:4 yrs:6 yrs)

Measurements:
Chest:
51.5(57:60:68.5:74)cm /
20(22½:23¾:27:29¼)in
Approximate length:
27(31:35:38:42)cm /
10¾(12¼:13¾:15:16½)in
(measured from the back
neck down)

Yarn:
3(4:5:6:7) balls of Dale of Norway/
Dalegarn Cotinga (aran/10-ply/
worsted); 50g/1¾oz/80m/88yd
Shown in Lys sand (light sand)
(2431), page 80 and Syren (lilac)
(5302), page 84

Suggested needles:
4mm (UK 8, US 6) and 4.5mm
(UK 7, US 7) circular needles,
40–60cm (16–24in) long;
4mm (UK 8, US 6) and 4.5mm
(UK 7, US 7) DPN

Tension (gauge):
21 sts and 30 rows to 10cm (4in)
in pattern on 4.5mm (UK 7,
US 7) needles
20 sts and 27 rows to 10cm (4in) in
st st on 4.5mm (UK 7, US 7) needles

PATTERN NOTES

The sweater is worked in rounds from the bottom up and the yoke is shaped with raglan decreases.
The body is worked in pattern, while the sleeves are knitted in st st.
The neck is finished off with a low ribbed border.
The pattern is shown in the chart on page 85.

BODY

On 4mm (UK 8, US 7) circular needles, cast on 108(120:128:144:156) sts and join to work in the round. Pm to mark beg of round. The round starts at the centre back.
Work 4cm (1½in) in k2, p2 rib, decreasing 0(0:2:0:0) sts evenly on the final round. 108(120:126:144:156) sts.

Change to 4.5mm (UK 7, US 7) needles.
Work in pattern following the chart, repeating the 6-st rep 18(20:21:24:26) times across the round until work measures approx. 18(20:23:25:28)cm / 7(7¾:9:9¾:11)in, ending on an even round.

SHAPE ARMHOLES

Next round: patt 24(24:30:30:36), cast (bind) off 6 sts for the sleeve, patt 48(54:60:66:72), cast (bind) off 6 sts for the second sleeve, patt to end. 96(108:114:132:144 sts).
Set the work aside and make the sleeves.

SLEEVES

On 4mm (UK 8, US 6) DPN, cast on 28(32:32:36:40) sts and join to work in the round. Pm to mark beg of round.
Work 3cm (1¼in) in k2, p2 rib.

Change to 4.5mm (UK 7, US 7) DPN.
Work the sleeves in rounds in st st until sleeve measures 2(3:3:4:5)cm / ¾(1¼:1¼:1½:2in) from end of rib.

Next round (inc): k1, m1l knit to last st, m1r, k1. 2 sts increased.

Repeat inc round every 2(3:3:4:5)cm / ¾(1¼:1¼:1½:2)in until you have increased a total of 5 times. 38(42:42:46:50) sts.
Cont in st st until the sleeve measures 19(22:25:28:32)cm / 7½(8¾:9¾:11:12¼)in from cast-on (bound-on) edge.

Rep last 2 rounds a total of 11(13:14:17:19) times, ending on a round without decreases and changing to DPN where necessary. 72(76:74:76:80) sts.

On the next round decrease 4(4:2:4:4) sts as follows:

Sizes 6 mths, 1 yr, 4 yrs and 6 yrs:
Patt to marker, sm, p1, sm, k2tog, patt to 2 sts before the next marker, skpo, sm, p1, sm, rep from * to * once more, patt to end.
68(72:-:72:76) sts.

Size 2 yrs:
Work 1 round, decreasing 1 stitch on each sleeve by working k2tog in the middle of the sleeve. -(-:72:-:-) sts.

All sizes:
Change to 4mm (UK 8, US 7) needles.
Work 2cm (¾in) in k2, p2 rib.
Cast (bind) off in rib using 4.5mm (UK 7, US 7) needles.

FINISHING
Darn in all the ends and sew the underarm seams.

CHART

Read the chart from right to left on all rounds; the sweater is worked in rounds.

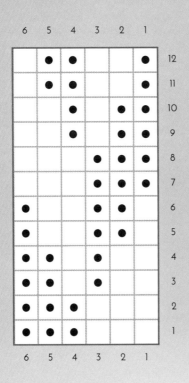

	knit
•	purl
	Pattern repeat

SVALA

Svala is an old Nordic name that has several meanings. If translated from Swedish it means 'cool', but in Denmark it was used by the Vikings to mean 'strength'. The name suits this top and dress well; the straps draw attention to the shoulders, showing the strength of the body, and the loose fit means that Svala is nice and cool to wear on a hot summer's day.

Because of its simple look, the pretty pattern on the back, the lace effect on the front and its light, summery feeling, Svala has become one of my absolute favourites.

Sizes:
1 yr(2 yrs:4 yrs:6 yrs)

Measurements:
Chest:
50(57:62:66)cm / 19¾(22½:24½:26)in (measured just below the chest)
Length of top:
18(20:22:25)cm / 7(7¾:8¾:9¾)in (from underarm)
Length of dress:
33(36:37:39)cm / 13(14¼:14½:15¼)in (from underarm)
Circumference at bottom edge:
82(86:93:100)cm / 32¼(33¾:36½:39½)in

Yarn:
Sandnes Merinoull (DK/8-ply/light worsted); 50g/1¾oz/105m/115yd
Shown in Gammelrosa (vintage pink) (4042), page 86 and Okker (ochre) (2035), page 90

Quantity, top:
3(4:5:5) balls
Quantity, dress:
5(5:6:7) balls

Suggested needles:
3mm (UK 11, US 2/3) and 3.5mm (UK 9/10, US 4) circular needles, 40–60cm (16–24in) long.
If desired, a pair of 3mm (UK 11, US 2/3) DPN for the i-cord straps

Tension (gauge):
22 sts and 30 rows to 10cm (4in) in st st on 3.5mm (UK 9/10, US 4) needles

Edge stitches:
Knit the first stitch through back loop. Slip the last stitch purlwise, with the yarn at the front of the work

PATTERN NOTES

Both the top and the dress are worked in rounds in st st from the bottom up to the armholes, then the front and back are worked in rows.

The top can be made quite plain without the frill, or with the frill to liven it up a bit.

There is a pretty lacy pattern on the back, which is shown in the chart on page 91.

The top and the dress fit loosely around the body and give plenty of room for movement.

Take care that your tension (gauge) does not become too loose when you are working in rows rather than rounds and go down a needle size if necessary.

BODY

On 3mm (UK 11, US 2/3) circular needles cast on 180(189:204:219) sts and join to work in the round. Pm to mark beg of round.

Work in st st until work measures 2cm (¾in).

Purl 1 round (fold edge).

Change to 3.5mm (UK 9/10, US 4) needles and continue in st st until work measures:

Top: 18(20:22:25)cm / 7(7¾:8¾: 9¾)in from the fold edge.

Dress: 33(36:37:39)cm 13(14¼:14½: 15¼)in from the fold edge.

Next round: knit, decreasing 70(63:68:73) sts evenly spaced. Decrease by working k2tog. 110(126:136:146) sts.

NOTE: On the next round you must cast (bind) off tightly in order to achieve the right circumference. It is a good idea to do this with a smaller needle. The top or dress fits loosely, but if you want it to fit the body more closely, you can decrease an extra 8 sts on each side as you cast off.

Cast (bind) off 20(24:26:29) sts, work st st over the next 15 sts (back), cast (bind) off 20(24:27:29), work 55(63:68:73) sts (front). Transfer the 15 sts of the back to scrap yarn and finish the front and back separately.

FRONT

Turn and work a purl row, remembering the edge stitches.

Next row (RS dec): edge st, skpo, knit to last 3 sts, k2tog, edge st. 2 sts decreased.

Rep last 2 rows another 3(4:5:6) times. 47(53:56:59) sts.

Continue in st st until work measures 5(6:7:8)cm / 2(2¼:2¾:3¼)in from divide, ending with a WS row.

FRILL VERSION:

If you would like to work a frill on your dress or top, work the next 2 rows as follows:

Next row (RS): edge st, purl (frill) to last st, edge st (this row marks the placement of the frill).

Next row: purl.

NO FRILL VERSION:
If you do not want frills, work 2 more rows in st st.

BOTH VERSIONS:
Change to 3mm (UK 11, US 2/3) needles
Next row (RS): edge st, skpo, k10, k2tog, k1, purl to last 16 sts, k1, skpo, k10, k2tog, edge st. 43(49:52:55) sts.
Next row: edge st, p13, knit to last 14 sts, p13, edge st.
Next row: edge st, skpo, k8, k2tog, k1, cast (bind) off 15(21:24:27) sts (1 st on RS needle after cast (bind) off), skpo, k8, k2tog, edge st. 12 sts rem each side.

Finish the two shoulders separately.
Next row (WS): edge st, purl across the shoulder to last st, edge st.
Next row: edge st, skpo, k6, k2tog, edge st. 10 sts.
Next row: edge st, purl to last st, edge st.
Next row: edge st, skpo, k4, k2tog, edge st. 8 sts.
Next row: edge st, purl to last st, edge st.
Next row: edge st, skpo, k2, k2tog, edge st. 6 sts.
Next row: edge st, purl to last st, edge st.

Cast (bind) off the shoulder purlwise on the RS.
With WS facing, rejoin the yarn to the second shoulder and complete in the same way.

BACK
On 3.5mm (UK 9/10, US 4) needles, rejoin yarn to 15 held sts of back.
Work the 15 sts of lace pattern following the chart. Note that the outermost stitch at each side of the chart is an edge st and must be worked as such.
WS rows are not charted and should be worked as purl with edge stitches.
Finish the chart with a WS row.

STRAPS
After working the chart, divide the remaining 14 sts into 4 i-cords, to be attached to the front. Make the i-cords individually on 3mm (UK 11, US 2/3) DPN, dividing as follows:

Knit 3 sts, transfer the remaining sts of the back to scrap yarn.
Work these 3 sts as an i-cord (see Techniques, page 11) until the cord measures 13cm (5in) or the desired length. Cast (bind) off.
Work the next 4 sts from the scrap yarn as follows: k2, k2tog. Continue working these stitches as an i-cord until it is the same length as the previous cord. Cast (bind) off.

Work the next 4 sts from the scrap yarn as follows: k2tog, k2. Continue working these stitches as an i-cord until it is the same length as the other cords. Cast (bind) off.
Work the last 3 sts of the back as an i-cord to the same length as the others. Cast (bind) off.

89

FRILL

Pick up 47(53:57:59) sts along the frill placement line.
Row 1: edge st, (kfb) to last 2 sts, k1, edge st.
Continue working the first and last sts as edge sts and the remainder of the frill in st st until work measures 4cm (1¾in), ending on a WS row.
Next row (RS): edge st, (yo, k2tog) to last 2 sts, k1, edge st.
Work 1 row purl and 1 row knit. On the next row (WS) cast (bind) off knitwise.

FINISHING

Darn in all the ends. Sew the fold edge of the front in place on the wrong side. Sew two straps in place on one shoulder and the remaining two on the other shoulder.

CHART

Work the chart from right to left on all rows; the wrong side rows are not shown in the chart and should simply be worked purl over all stitches.

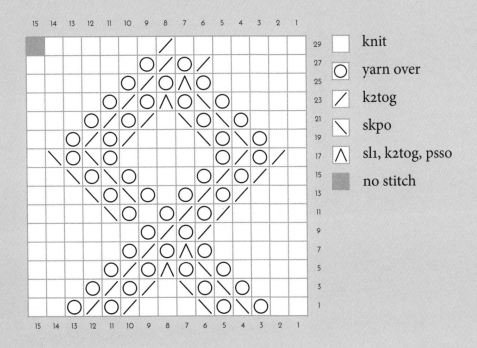

☐	knit
O	yarn over
╱	k2tog
╲	skpo
∧	sl1, k2tog, psso
▨	no stitch

EVERYDAY

When I designed this suit, I felt it was important that it should be unisex, fit well and allow freedom of movement. It should also be able to grow with the child, so the knitter would get a good stretch for all the time invested in the project.

In my experience, children love suits. They are comfortable to wear, do not separate and leave bare skin anywhere, and provide freedom of movement for children who want to climb and crawl over everything. I think I succeeded in giving this suit just the right fit with plenty of fine details, such as extra-long ribbed borders on the legs, which can be folded down when the child grows. Shaping with German short rows provides plenty of room for the child's bottom, and decreasing in rib over the small of the back allows it to follow the curve of the child's body. Ties at the waist pull the suit in more tightly and give it more shape. Openings at both the front and one shoulder mean there is plenty of space and make it easier for the child to put on.

Everyday is full of fun techniques and details and offers the knitter interest and variety.

Sizes:
9 mths(1 yr:2 yrs:4 yrs:6 yrs)

Measurements:
Chest:
45(48:55:58:62)cm /
17¾(19:21¾:22¾:24½)in
Hips:
52(55:61:65:70)cm /
20½(21¾:24:25½:27½)in
Inside leg:
26(30:33:40:43)cm /
10¼(11¾:13:15¾:17)in

Yarn:
3(4:4:5:6) balls of Sandnes Tynn Merinoull (4-ply/fingering);
50g/1¾oz/175m/191yd
Shown in Støvet koral (dusty coral) (4214)

Buttons:
3(3:4:4:5), 15mm (⅝in) diameter
3(3:3:3:3), 13mm (½in) diameter

Suggested needles:
3mm (UK 11, US 2/3) and 2 sets of 3.5mm (UK 9/10, US 4) circular needles, 40–60cm (16–24in) long;
3mm (UK 11, US 2/3) and 3.5mm (UK 9/10, US 4) DPN

Tension (gauge):
26 sts and 36 rows to 10cm (4in) in st st on 3.5mm (UK 9/10, US 4) needles

Edge stitches:
Edge stitches are worked knit on all rows

PATTERN NOTES

The trouser suit is worked from the bottom up. The legs are worked individually in rounds, then the pieces are joined together and you continue in rounds. Lastly the work is divided into front and back. The suit is worked mainly in stocking (stockinette) stitch, but includes fine details, such as the rib on the back, the waist tie and the buttonhole band on the front.
It is a really good idea to measure the inside length of your child's legs so you can make adjustments if necessary. The suit is nice and roomy at the back, where it is shaped with German short rows, and then made narrower with ribbing.

LEGS

On 3mm (UK 11, US 2/3) DPN, cast on 48(52:54:58:60) sts and join to work in the round. Pm to mark beg of round.
Work 6(8:8:8:8)cm / 2¼(3¼:3¼:3¼:3¼)in, in k1, p1, rib.

Change to 3.5mm (UK 9/10, US 4) needles.
Work in st st until work measures 2(2:2:3:3)cm / ¾(¾:¾:1¼:1¼)in from the rib border, then increase on each side of the start of the round as follows:
Inc round: k1, m1l, k to last st, m1r, k1. 2 sts increased.
Repeat inc round a total of 8(8:10:10:11) times, working 2(2:2:3:3)cm / ¾(¾:¾:1¼: 1¼)in between the increases.
64(68:74:78:82) sts.

Continue in st st until work measures 26(30:33:40:43)cm / 10¼(11¾:13; 15¾:17)in or the desired length from cast-on (bound-on) edge.
Make a second leg to match the first.

JOIN PIECES TOGETHER

Work the legs on to the same needle. Make sure the increases turn in towards each other.
Round 1: knit across 64(68:74:78:82) sts of the left leg, cast on 2(2:3:3:4) sts, pm (centre front marker), cast on 2(2:3:3:4) sts, knit across 64(68:74:78:82) sts of the right leg, cast on 4(4:6:6:8) sts, pm to mark beg of round.
136(144:160:168:180) sts.

Work in st st until work measures 15(15:17:20:21)cm / 6(6:6¾: 7¾:8¼)in from the crotch up. It is a good idea to measure your own child to check that this will fit, as some children are longer in the lower part of the body than others. The work should now reach the child's hips.

German short rows and rib

Now work German short rows to create extra room at the back.

Sizes 9 mths and 1 yr:

K to 1 st before beg of round, turn.
P25, turn.
K to 22 sts after beg of round, turn.
P to 22 sts after beg of round, turn.
K to 18 sts after beg of round, turn.
P to 18 sts after beg of round, turn.

K to 14 sts after beg of round, turn.
P to 14 sts after beg of round, turn.
K to 10 sts after beg of round, turn.
P to 10 sts after beg of round, turn.
K to 6 sts after beg of round, turn.
P to 1 st after beg of round, turn.

Sizes 2 yrs and 4 yrs:
K to 1 st before beg of round, turn.
P32, turn.
K to 26 sts after beg of round, turn.
P to 28 sts after beg of round, turn.
K to 22 sts after beg of round, turn.
P to 24 sts after beg of round, turn.
K to 18 sts after beg of round, turn.
P to 20 sts after beg of round, turn.
K to 14 sts after beg of round, turn.
P to 16 sts after beg of round, turn.
K to 10 sts after beg of round, turn.
P to 1 st after beg of round, turn.

Size 6 yrs:
K to 1 st before beg of round, turn.
P38, turn.
K to 30 sts after beg of round, turn.
P to 34 sts after beg of round, turn.
K to 27 sts after beg of round, turn.
P to 30 sts after beg of round, turn.
K to 23 sts after beg of round, turn.
P to 26 sts after beg of round, turn.
K to 19 sts after beg of round, turn.
P to 22 sts after beg of round, turn.
K to 15 sts after beg of round, turn.
P to 1 st after beg of round, turn.

All sizes:
Work 2 rounds in st st,
remembering to knit the turning
stitches together every time
you turn.

Sizes 9 months and 1 yr: (p2tog,
k2tog) 3 times, p2tog, pm, k to last
16 sts, (p2tog, k2tog) 4 times.

Sizes 2 yrs and 4 yrs: (p2tog,
k2tog) 3 times, p2tog, pm, k to last
20 sts, (p2tog, k2tog) 5 times.

Size 6 yrs: (p2tog, k2tog) 3 times,
p2tog, pm, k to last 20 sts, pm,
(p2tog, k2tog) 5 times.

All sizes:
119(127:143:151:163) sts.
Work in rib between the two
markers and st st over the other
sts until the ribbing measures
2cm (¾in).

TIE

Make the casing for the waistline
cord. Thread a strand of
contrasting yarn through all the
stitches of the round, without
taking them off the needle. This
strand will be used to make
it easier to pick up the sts at
a later stage.
Work 3 rounds in st st.
Set the work aside.

With a new 3.5mm (UK 9/10, US 4)
circular needle, starting at the beg
of the round, pick up all the sts
along the strand of yarn from the
wrong side. Replace markers at
centre front and beg of round.

Work 3 rounds on these stitches
as follows:
Round 1: work all sts as
they present.
Round 2: work rib and st st to 5 sts
before the centre front marker,
yo, k2tog, k6, k2tog, yo, work in
st st and rib over the remainder of
the round.
Round 3: work rib over the rib sts
and st st over the remainder.

On the next round hold the sts of
the two parts of the casing together
with RS facing out and use a third
needle to work together pairs
of stitches, one from each part,
keeping rib and st st pattern as set.

Continue in st st and rib until
ribbing measures 5cm (2in) in total.
Work in st st over all sts until
work measures 29(31:34:38:41)cm
/ 11½(12¼:13½:15:16¼)in from the
crotch (measured at the front).

Divide the work into front and
back as follows and finish each
part separately.
Knit to 33(35:39:41:44) sts before
the centre front marker, cast
(bind) off 6 sts, knit until there are
30(32:36:38:41) sts on the needle
(left front), pm. Knit across the
following 24(26:30:32:35) sts (right
front), cast (bind) off 6 sts, knit
to start of round and break off
the yarn.
Transfer all the 53(57:65:69:75) sts
of the back to the same needle and
work the back first.

BACK

Join yarn on right side and work
2 rows stocking (stockinette) stitch
over the 53(57:65:69 75) sts of
the back.
Next row (RS): edge st, skpo,
k to last 3 sts, k2tog, edge st.
2 sts decreased.

Continue decreasing in this way
on every right side row a total of
3(3:4:5:6) times. 47(51:57:59:63) sts.

Work straight in st st until work
measures 12(13:14:15:16)cm /
4¾(5:5½:6:6¼)in from the armhole.
Set the middle 29(31:35:35:37) sts
aside and continue to work the
outer 9(10:11:12:13) sts (including
edge sts) of each shoulder
individually until shoulder
measures 14(15:16:17:18)cm /
5½(6:6¼:6¾:7)in, measured from
the armhole.

On the left shoulder, work a further
1cm (⅜in) in garter stitch (knit
all rows).
Cast (bind) off knitwise on the
wrong side.
Cast (bind) off the stitches of the
right shoulder.

LEFT FRONT

With the RS facing, join the yarn at
the armhole and knit to 6 sts before
the centre front marker, pm, k6.
Set the remaining 24(26:30:32:35)
sts of the right front aside.
Turn the work and work a WS row
as follows:

Next row (WS): k6 (buttonhole band), purl to last st, edge st.

BUTTONHOLE BAND
NOTE: The outer 6 sts form the buttonhole band, which is worked in garter stitch at the same time as the front.
Position a total of 2(2:3:3:4) buttonholes over the 9(10:11: 12:13)cm / 3½(4:4¼:4¾:5)in of the front.
The buttonholes should be evenly spaced, with the bottom one approx. 1cm (⅜in) from the edge. You will be making another buttonhole in the neck border at the end, so take care not to place the top buttonhole too close to the edge of the neck. Make the buttonholes on RS rows by knitting to last 4 sts, cast (bind) off 2 sts, k2. On the WS, cast on 2 sts over the cast-(bound-)off sts.

SHAPE ARMHOLES
Dec row (RS): edge st, skpo, k to end of row. 1 st decreased.
Work 1 WS row.
Continue decreasing 1 st on each RS row as set a total of 3(3:4:5:6) times. 27(29:32:33:35) sts.
Work in rows in st st and garter stitch until the piece measures 9(10:11:12:13)cm / 3½(4:4¼:4¾:5)in from the armhole, remembering to place buttonholes as you go, ending with a WS row.

DIVIDE FOR NECK
Next row (RS): edge st, k8(9:10:11:12), transfer the next 18(19:21:21:22) sts to scrap yarn for neck, turn and p8(9:10:11:12), edge st.
Work in rows in st st with edge sts until work measures 14(15:16:17:18) cm / 5½(6:6¼:6¾:7)in from the armhole.
Knit 2 rows.
Next row (RS): edge st, k2(2:3:3:4), k2tog, yo, k4(5:5:6:6) (1 buttonhole made).
Knit 2 rows and cast (bind) off knitwise on the WS.

RIGHT FRONT
On 3.5mm (UK 9/10, US 4) needles, cast on 6 sts. Place a marker and knit across the 24(26:30:32:35) sts set aside for the right front. 30(32:36:38:41) sts.
Next row (WS): edge st, p to last 6 sts, k6.
Next row (RS): k6, k to last 3 sts, k2tog, edge st. 1 st decreased.
Continue decreasing 1 st on each RS row as set a total of 3(3:4:5:6) times. 27(29:32:33:35) sts.

Work in rows in st st and garter stitch until the piece measures 9(10:11:12:13)cm / 3½(4:4¼:4¾:5)in from the armhole, remembering to place buttonholes as you go, ending with a WS row.

DIVIDE FOR NECK
Next row (WS): edge st, p8(9:10:11:12), transfer the next 18(19:21:21:22) sts to scrap yarn for neck, turn and k8(9:10:11:12), edge st.
Work in rows in st st with edge sts until work measures 14(15:16: 17:18)cm / 5½(6:6¼:6¾:7)in from the armhole.
Cast (bind) off.

NECK BORDER

Graft the right shoulder seam together.

With RS facing, rejoin yarn and slip the 18(19:21:21:22) sts on scrap yarn for the right front neck to a 3mm (UK 11, US 2/3) needle and knit across, pick up and knit sts up the right front shoulder (skipping approx. every third stitch), pick up and knit sts down the right back shoulder (skipping approx. every third stitch), slip the 29(31:35:35:37) sts on scrap yarn for the back neck to the needle and knit across, then pick up and knit sts up the left back shoulder, making sure you have the same number of stitches on each shoulder.

Knit 4 more rows.

Cast (bind) off purlwise on the RS.

With RS facing, rejoin yarn and pick up and knit sts down the left front shoulder (skipping approx. every third stitch and making sure you have the same number as on the right), then slip the 18(19:21:21:22) sts on scrap yarn for the left front neck to a 3mm (UK 11, US 2/3) needle and knit across.

Knit 1 more row.

On the next RS row make two buttonholes, one in the front edge of the buttonhole band and one on the shoulder next to the second buttonhole. The buttonhole on the shoulder is worked in line with the second buttonhole by casting off 2 sts and casting on 2 new sts on the following row.

The buttonhole on the front is made by working knit to last 4 sts, cast (bind) off 2 sts, k2.

On the next row, cast on 2 new sts over the cast-(bound-)off sts.

Knit 2 rows and cast (bind) off purlwise on the right side.

ARMHOLE EDGES

With 3mm (UK 11, US 2/3) needles pick up and knit 2 sts for every 3 rows around the armhole edge.

The right armhole edge is worked in rounds:

Work 4 rounds in garter stitch.

Cast (bind) off knitwise on the next round.

The left armhole edge is worked in rows:

Pick up and knit the same number of sts on the right side.

Knit 4 rows.

Cast (bind) off purlwise on the next row (RS).

FINISHING

Sew up the crotch seam and sew the button band in place on the WS. Sew the buttons on the button band and at the shoulder. Make an i-cord (see Techniques, page 11). Work until the i-cord measures 75(78:85:88:92)cm / 29½(30¾:33½:34¾:36¼)in or the desired length. Darn in all the ends and thread the cord through the casing.

CHARMING

When I started designing for this book, I was quite certain that I wanted to include some patterns with beads. I was very inspired by the many pretty woven bead bracelets people make, not only by their lovely motifs but also the sheen and simplicity of the beads. Small glass beads produced the perfect effect for my knitting, I thought – not too overwhelming, yet adding beauty and contrast.

So I began knitting lots of samples to see how the beads looked, depending on which method I used to insert them, and it will certainly not be the last time I do so. In this pattern you can give free rein to your creativity and draw inspiration from lovely motifs, colours, and so on. This enables you to achieve exactly the effect you want by playing around with colours of both the knitting and the beads. What I particularly love about this pattern is the perfect balance between the simple stocking (stockinette) stitch and the abundance of beads, and the elegant look.

Just like its name, it is simply charming.

#CHARMING TOP #CHARMING DRESS

Sizes:
1 yr(2 yrs:3–4 yrs:5–6 yrs)

To fit chest:
48(53:58:61)cm / 19(20¾:22¾:24)in

Measurements:
Top:
Chest:
64(68:74:77)cm / 25¼(26¾:29¼:
30¼)in
Length:
30(34:38:42)cm / 11¾(13½:15:
16¼)in (measured from the back
neck down)

Dress:
Chest:
64(68:74:77)cm / 25¼(26¾:29¼:
30¼)in
Length:
42(46:49:52)cm / 16½(18:19¼:20½)in
(measured from the back
neck down)
Bottom edge circumference:
74(80:99:104)cm / 29¼(31½:39:41)in

Yarn:
Sandnes Alpakka Silke (4-ply/
fingering) (4-ply/fingering);
50g/1¾oz/200m/218½yd
Shown in Gammelrosa (vintage
pink) (4331)

Quantity, top:
2(3:3:4) balls
Quantity, dress:
3(4:4:4) balls

**Other materials (both dress
and top):**
238(238:252:266) beads,
3.8–4.5mm diameter
1 button, between 10–15cm
(4–6in) diameter
Thin nylon thread or beading needle

Suggested needles:
2.5mm (UK 13/12, US 1/2) and 3mm
(UK 11, US 2/3) circular needles,
40–60cm (16–24in) long;
2.5mm (UK 13/12, US 1/2) and 3mm
(UK 11, US 2/3) DPN

Tension (gauge):
27 sts and 38 rows to 10cm (4in) in
st st on 3mm needles

Edge stitches:
Knit the first stitch through the back
loop. Slip the last st purlwise, with
the yarn at the front of the work

PATTERN NOTES

Both the top and the dress are worked from the top down, at first in rows to form the back neck opening, then in rounds.

The pattern is worked in st st with raglan increases and extra increases on the front.

It fits loosely but has tight-fitting three-quarter length sleeves.

It has beads on the front.

BEADS

Work the beads in one by one on the stitches of the front. When increasing in rows where beads are to be added, always add two more beads on every second row, so the new stitches are also worked with beads. The beads are worked in on both right side and wrong side rows.

It is fun to play about with beads and see what different effects they can create. You can make the beaded part in a single colour, in stripes or maybe even in a pattern.

How to knit the beads in

There are several things you can use to help you insert the beads into the work. I used a beading needle that I cut open at one end, leaving the other end closed. You can also use a thin nylon thread. Insert the nylon thread/beading needle through the stitch, slip the stitch off the needle, leaving it hanging from the thread/beading needle.

Bring the ends of the thread/beading needle together and thread on a bead.

Pull the bead down over the stitch, put the stitch back on the left needle and remove the thread/beading needle, then knit or purl the stitch, depending on whether you are working a right or wrong side row.

YOKE

On 2.5mm (UK 13/12, US 1/2) circular needles, cast on 82(82:86:90) sts and knit 3 rows (remembering edge st at each side). The first row is a right side row.

Place markers for raglan as follows:
Next row (WS): edge st, k14(14:15:16) (back 1), pm, k1 (raglan), pm, k10(10:10:10) (right sleeve), pm, k1 (raglan), pm, k28(28:30:32) (front), pm, k1 (raglan), pm, k10(10:10:10) (left sleeve), pm, k1 (raglan), pm, k14(14:15:16) (back 2), edge st.

Now you will add beads on the front between the two raglan sts, while also working the raglan increases.

Change to 3mm (UK 11, US 2/3) needles and continue in st st as follows:

Next row (RS inc): edge st, k to marker, m1r, sm, k1 (raglan), sm, m1l, k to marker, m1r, sm, k1 (raglan), sm, m1l, knit across front sts to marker, inserting a bead on each st, m1r, sm, k1 (raglan), sm, m1l, k to marker, m1r, sm, k1 (raglan), sm, m1l, k to last st, edge st. 8 sts increased.

Next row (WS): edge st, *purl to marker, sm, p1 (raglan), sm* rep from * to * once more, purl the 30(30:32:34) sts of the front, inserting a bead on each one, sm, purl to last st (slipping markers), edge st.

Repeat last 2 rows, adding beads on both RS and WS rows, until you have worked a total of 7 rows with beads. 114(114:118:122) sts.
Work 1 WS row without beads.

Next row (RS inc): edge st, k to marker, m1r, sm, k1 (raglan), sm, m1l, k to marker, m1r, sm, k1 (raglan), sm, m1l, knit into front and back loops of all 36(36:38:40) sts of the front, m1r, sm, k1 (raglan), sm, m1l, k to marker, m1r, sm, k1 (raglan), sm, m1l, k to last st, edge st.
There are now 158(158:164:170) sts on the needle and 74(74:78:82) sts on the front.
Next row: purl.

Next row (RS inc): edge st, *k to marker, m1r, sm, k1 (raglan), sm, m1l*, rep from * to * 3 more times, k to last st, edge st. 8 sts increased.
Next row: purl.
Rep last 2 rows another 4 times. 198(198:204:210) sts.

JOIN INTO THE ROUND
Next row (RS inc): *k to marker, m1r, sm, k1 (raglan), sm, m1l*, rep from * to * 3 more times, k to last st, knit last st together with

first st to join into the round and pm to mark beg of round.
Next round: knit.

Continue in rounds in st st with raglan increases on every even round until you have increased a total of 16(19:21:22) times since the start of the work. Finish with a non-increase round. 245(269:291:305) sts.

DIVIDE SLEEVES AND BODY
Set the sts for the sleeves aside as follows:
Next round: removing markers as you go, k to marker, k1, transfer 42(48:52:54) sts to scrap yarn, cast on 8 new sts at the underarm, k1, k to next marker, k1, transfer 42(48:52:54) sts to scrap yarn, cast on 8 new sts at the underarm, k to end. 177(189:203:213) sts.

This means the raglan sts are part of the back and front.
Work 1 round knitting the first and last of the 8 new underarm sts together with a st of the back or front. 173(185:199:209) sts.

If you are making the dress, on the same round place a marker at the centre of the new sts cast on at each underarm.

TOP
Continue working in rounds in st st until work measures 30(34:38:42)cm / 11¾(13½:15:16½)in measured from the back neck, or until the top is 1cm (⅜in)

shorter than the desired length.
Change to 2.5mm (UK 13/12,
US 1/2) needles.

Round 1: purl.
Round 2: knit.
Work last 2 rounds once more.

Cast (bind) off loosely purlwise
with 3mm (UK 11, US 2/3) needles.

DRESS

Work 2cm (¾in) in st st.
Next round (inc): *k to 1 st before
marker, m1r, k2, m1l*, rep from * to
* once more, k to end of round.
4 sts increased.

Continue increasing at both
markers every 4(4:2:2)cm /
1½(1½:¾:¾)in until you have
increased a total of 7(8:17:18) times.
201(217:267:281) sts.

Continue working in rounds
in st st until work measures
42(46:49:52)cm / 16½(18:19¼:20½)
in or 1cm (⅜in) shorter than the
desired length.

Change to 2.5mm (UK 13/12,
US 1/2) needles.

Round 1: purl.
Round 2: knit.
Work last 2 rounds once more.
Cast (bind) off loosely purlwise
with 3mm (UK 11, US 2/3) needles.

SLEEVES
Transfer the 42(48:52:54) sts from
the scrap yarn to 3mm (UK 11,
US 2/3) DPN and cast on 6 new sts
at the underarm. Place a marker
for the start of the round at the
centre of the new cast on sts.
48(54:58:60) sts.
Work in rounds in st st until work
measures 3cm (1¼)in.

Next round (dec): k2tog, k to last
2 sts, skpo. 2 sts decreased.
Decrease every 3cm (1¼in) a total
of 4 times.

Work until sleeve measures
12(13:15:17)cm / 4¾(5:6:6¾)in.

Change to 2.5cm (UK 13/12,
US 1/2) DPN.

Round 1: purl.
Round 2: knit.
Work last 2 rounds once more.

Cast (bind) off loosely purlwise
with 3mm (UK 11, US 2/3) needles.
Make a second sleeve in the
same way.

FINISHING
Crochet a loop at the back neck
and sew a button on the other side.
Darn in all the ends.
Wash according to instructions on
yarn and dry flat, stretching the
skirt out (see 'A Good Start: Care' –
page 14).

QUILTED

This cardigan just had to be called Quilted. The structure of the pattern looks a little like quilted bedspreads with a decorative, apparently three-dimensional pattern. This texture is created by slipping stitches with the yarn in front of the work at staggered intervals and then knitting the loose strand together with a stitch above. It is a very easy pattern to knit; you will soon pick up the rhythm and enjoy the fun and variety.

Quilted is a really captivating project and I could hardly bear to put it down when I was making it for the first time. The cardigan is perfect for both boys and girls and can function as both a jacket and a cardigan because of the warm yarn and the firm structure.

#QUILTED CARDIGAN

Sizes:
3 mths(6 mths:1 yr:2 yrs:4 yrs:6 yrs)

Measurements:
Chest:
48(52:58:65:68:72)cm /
19(20½:22¾:25½:26¾:28¼)in
Length:
24(28:33:37:39:43)cm /
9½(11:13:14½:15¼:17)in
(measured from the back
neck down)

Yarn:
2(3:3:4:4:5) balls of Du Store Alpakka
Mini Sterk (4-ply/fingering);
50g/1¾oz/166m/181yd
Shown in Natural (806)

Buttons:
6(7:8:9:9:10)

Suggested needles:
3mm (UK 11, US 2/3) circular
needles, 40–60cm (16–24in) long

NOTE: If you work with a less
stretchy yarn than originally
suggested, you should possibly work
the rib on 2.5mm (UK 13/12, US 1/2)
needles so the rib border will not be
too loose.

Tension (gauge):
29 sts and 34 rows to 10cm (4in)
in pattern on 3mm (UK 11,
US 2/3) needles

Edge stitches:
The outermost stitch at each end
of the row is an edge stitch and is
worked knit on all rows

PATTERN NOTES

The cardigan is worked in rows from the bottom up. The yoke is shaped with raglan decreases. The cardigan is worked with a lattice pattern on the sleeves and body, but also looks fine with sleeves in stocking (stockinette) stitch.

LATTICE PATTERN

Row 1 (WS): purl.
Row 2: k2, *sl3pwyif, k1*, repeat from * to * to end of row.
Row 3: purl.
Row 4: k2, *k1, k1 uls, k2*, repeat from * to * to end of row.
Row 5: purl.
Row 6: *sl3pwyif, k1*, repeat from * to * to last 2 sts, k2.
Row 7: purl.
Row 8: *k1, k1 uls, k2*; repeat from * to * to last 2 sts, k2.

Repeat rows 1–8.

BODY

On 3mm (UK 11, US 2/3) needles, cast on 136(148:164:184:192:204) sts.
Row 1 (WS): edge st, (k1, p1) to last st, edge st.
Row 2: edge st, (p1, k1) to last st, edge st.

Continue working rows in rib in this way until border measures 2cm (¾in), ending on a RS row.

Next row (WS): edge st, work lattice pattern (as above) to last st, edge st. Continue to work in lattice pattern until work measures approx. 15(16:19:22:23:26)cm / 6(6¼:7¼:8¾:9:10¼)in or desired length for body (longer rather than shorter), ending with a row 4 or row 8 of the pattern and taking a note of this to match sleeve cast-(bound-)off.

SHAPE ARMHOLES
Next row (WS): edge st, p26(29:33:38:40:43), cast (bind) off 12 sts, p until there are 58(64:72:82:86:92) sts on the needle after cast-(bound-)off, cast (bind) off 12 sts, p26(29:33:38:40:43), edge st.
112(124:140:160:168:180) sts.
Set the work aside and make the sleeves.

SLEEVES

Next row (WS): edge st, work in lattice pattern to last st, edge st.
Continue in pattern with edge sts at each side until work measures 2(2:2:2:2.5:3)cm / ¾(¾:¾:¾:1:1¼)in from ribbed border.

Next row (RS inc): edge st, m1l, work lattice pattern to last st, m1r, edge st. 2 sts increased.

Increase in this way on RS rows a total of 5(7:9:9:9:9) times with 2(2:2:2.5:3)cm / ¾(¾:¾:¾:1:1¼) in between increase rows. Work the new sts in st st and then into the pattern when possible. 50(58:62:66:70:74) sts.

Continue in pattern without shaping until the sleeve measures 16(19:22:26:30:34)cm / 6¼(7½:8¾:10¼:11¾:13½)in from cast-on (bound-on) edge.

SHAPE SLEEVECAP
Cast (bind) off for the armhole on row 1 or row 5 of the pattern as noted on the body, by casting off the first and last 7 sts, including the edge sts. 36(44:48:52:56:60) sts. Set the sleeve aside and make a second sleeve in the same way.

JOIN BODY AND SLEEVES
Next row (RS): edge st, *patt to cast-(bound-)off sts, pm, knit first st of sleeve, pm, patt across sleeve sts to last st, pm, knit last st of sleeve*, rep from * to * once more, patt to last st, edge st. 184(212:236:264:280:300) sts.

Work one WS row, purling sts between markers.
Next row (RS dec): edge st, *patt to 2 sts before marker, skpo, sm, k1, sm, k2tog*, rep from * to * 3 more times, patt to last st, edge st.

Repeat dec row every RS row a total of 8(11:14:17:19:21) times. 120(124:124:128:128:132) sts. Work 1 WS row.

SHAPE NECK
Next row (RS): cast (bind) off 3(3:3:4:4:4) sts, patt to end, working raglan decreases as set. 109(113:113:116:116:120) sts.
Next row: cast (bind) off 3(3:3:4:4:4), patt to end. 106(110:110:112:112:116) sts.
Next row: cast (bind) off 2(2:2:3:3:3) sts, patt to end, working raglan decreases as set. 96(100:100:101:101:105) sts.
Next row: cast (bind) off 2(2:2:3:3:3) sts, patt to end. 94(98:98:98:98:102) sts.
Next row: cast (bind) off 2 sts, patt to end, working raglan decreases as set. 84(88:88:88:88:92) sts.
Next row: cast (bind) off 2 sts, patt to end. 82(86:86:86:86:90) sts.
Next row: cast (bind) off 1(1:1:2: 2:2) sts, patt to end, working raglan decreases as set. 73(77:77:76:76:80) sts.
Next row: cast (bind) off 1(1:1:2:2:2) sts, patt to end. 72(76:76:74:74:78) sts.
Next row: cast (bind) off 1 st, patt to end, working raglan decreases as set. 63(67:67:65:65:69) sts.
Next row: cast (bind) off 1 st, patt to end. 62(66:66:64:64:68) sts.

Cut yarn, leaving a long tail.

NECK

With RS facing, pick up and knit 9(9:9:12:12:12) sts along the neck edge along the sts just cast (bind) off on right side of neck, knit across sts on needle, then pick up and knit 9(9:9:12:12:12) sts along the left neck cast-(bound-)off edge. 80(84:84:88:88:92) sts.
Next row (WS): edge st, (p1, k1) to last st, edge st.
Work 2cm (¾in) in rib and cast (bind) off in rib.

BUTTON BAND

With RS facing, pick up and knit sts along the left front, skipping approx. every fourth stitch, making sure you end up with a multiple of 2+1.
Work 2cm (¾in) in k1, p1 rib to last st, k1.

Mark placement for 6(7:8:9:9:10) buttons, the first one 1cm (⅜in) from the neck edge and the bottom one 1cm (⅜in) from the cast-on (bound-on) edge, with the remainder evenly spaced in between.

BUTTONHOLE BAND

Work in the same way as the button band along the right front, but after working 1cm (⅜in) in rib make 6(7:8:9:9:10) buttonholes to correspond with markers on RS rows.
Make buttonholes by working k2tog or p2tog as the stitches show, yo.

FINISHING

Join the sleeve seams and the armhole edges. Darn in all the ends and sew buttons to the button band.

QUILTED SHORTS

The lovely quilted cardigan had to have a pair of shorts to go with it to complete the outfit. I absolutely love knitted shorts for children; there is something beautiful and nostalgic about a pair of chubby legs with grazed skin, bruises and home-made shorts.

It is not just that the Quilted Shorts are easy and quick to knit, the pattern is also fun and varied. This is a really good project for beginners and for experienced knitters who want to add a bit of spice to knitting while watching TV.

The Quilted Shorts are nice for both boys and girls and you can create different looks by replacing the knitted tie at the waist with a leather cord, a strip of lace or something quite different.

Sizes:
3 mths(6 mths:1 yr:2 yrs:4 yrs)

Measurements:
Hips:
49(51:54:57:60)cm /
19¾(20:21¼:22½:23½)in
Length:
18(19.5:22:22:24.5)cm /
7(7½:8¼:8½:9½in)
(measured from the fold edge to the crotch)

Yarn:
2(2:2:2:2) balls of Du Store Alpakka Mini Sterk (4-ply/fingering); 50g/1¾oz/166m/181yd
Shown in Grå melert (grey marl) (822)

Suggested needles:
3mm (UK 11, US 2/3) circular needles, 40cm (16in) long;
2.5mm (UK 13/12, US 1/2) DPN

Tension (gauge):
29 sts and 34 rows to 10cm (4in) in pattern on 3mm (UK 11, US 2/3) needles

PATTERN NOTES

The shorts are worked in rounds from the top down. They are knitted in a lattice pattern, but with edges in st st, and pulled tight at the waist with a cord or elastic.

LATTICE PATTERN

Row 1: knit.
Row 2: k2, *sl3pwyif, k1*, repeat from * to * to end of round.
Row 3: knit.
Row 4: k2, *k1, k1 uls, k2*, repeat from * to * to end of round.
Row 5: knit.
Row 6: *sl3pwyif, k1 *, repeat from * to * to last 2 sts, k2.
Row 7: knit.
Row 8: *k1, k1 uls, k2*, repeat from * to * to last 2 sts, k2.

Repeat rows 1–8.

SHORTS

On 3mm (UK 11, US 2/3) circular needles, cast on 142(150:158:166:174) sts and join to work in the round. Pm to mark beg of round.

Work in st st until work measures 2cm (¾in).
Purl 1 round (fold edge).
Work 1cm (⅜in) st st.

Next round: k32(34:36:38:40), yo, k2tog, k2, k2tog, yo, k to end of round.
Continue in st st for a further 1cm (⅜in) and then purl another round.

Next round: work 70(74:78:82:86) sts from row 1 of lattice pattern, pm, p1, pm, work 70(74:78:82:86) sts from row 1 of lattice pattern, pm, p1, pm.
Last round sets pattern placement. Work as set, slipping markers as you go until the patterned section measures 12(13:15:16:18)cm / 4¾(5:6:6¼:7)in, taking care to purl the single stitch between the markers.

Cast (bind) off for the legs as follows:
Cast (bind) off 18(18:18:24:24) sts, pattern until there are 34(38:42:34:38) sts on the needle then transfer these to scrap yarn, cast (bind) off 37(37:37:49:49) sts, pattern until there are 34(38:42:34:38) sts on the needle, cast (bind) off 19(19:19:25:25) sts.

Finish the two parts of the crotch separately in rows as follows, purling all WS rows.

BACK

With RS facing, rejoin yarn to one set of 34(38:42:34:38) sts and cast (bind) off 3 sts at the beg of each row a total of 2(4:4:2:4) times, working the remaining sts in pattern. 28(26:30:28:26) sts.

Cast (bind) off 2 sts at the beg of each row a total of 8(8:10:8:8) times, working the remaining sts in pattern. 12(10:10:12:10) sts.

Work st st over these
12(10:10:12:10) sts for 1cm (⅜in)
then cast (bind) off, or set the sts
aside to graft together with the sts
of the front at the end.
Work the front in the same way.

LEG BORDERS

With 2.5mm (UK 13/12, US 1/2)
DPN pick up stitches all the way
round the leg opening, skipping
approx. every third stitch.
Work 2cm (¾in) in st st, then
1 round purl and then another 2cm
(¾in) st st.

Cast (bind) off knitwise. Take care
to cast (bind) off loosely, so that the
leg opening does not get too small.
Work the border on the second leg
in the same way.

FINISHING
Fold over the edges of the legs and
waistband and sew them into place
on the wrong side.
Sew or graft the crotch
seam together.
Make an i-cord or insert another
cord at the waist (see Techniques,
page 11).

ELINOR

I had an idea about wanting to design a suit that could be worn by very small babies and also by bigger girls. It needed to be very simple, with small, fine details and plenty of room for movement. I knew it was going to be knitted in a silk or a silk blend, as it would fall nicely and have a beautiful, glossy look.

The end result was Elinor. The feminine look of the design is brought out by the close-fitting top and the extra width in the bottom part, as well as a lovely dress-like fall, not to mention the pretty lace pattern along the raglans. So, despite the stocking (stockinette) stitch body, Elinor involves many techniques and details that make it fun to knit, such as the piping over the hips.

The detail of the long button fastening down the spine make the back look as pretty as the front (see page 119).

Sizes:
3 mths(6 mths:12 mths:18 mths:2 yrs)

Measurements:
Chest:
43(46:48:52:55)cm /
17(18:19:20½:21¾)in
Length:
30(34:38:43:47)cm /
11¾(13½:15:17:18½)in
(measured from the back neck
to the crotch)

Yarn:
3(3:3:4:4) balls of Sandnes
Alpakka Silke (4-ply/fingering);
50g/1¾oz/200m/218½yd
Shown in Sand (2521) page 116 and
Vinrød (wine) (4554) page 119

Buttons:
6(7:7:8:8), 13–15mm (½–
⅝in) diameter

Suggested needles:
2.5mm (UK 13/12, US 1/2) and 3mm
(UK 11, US 2/3) circular needles,
40–60cm (16–24in) long;
2.5mm (UK 13/12, US 1/2) and
3mm (UK 11, US 2/3) DPN

Tension (gauge):
28 sts and 38 rows to 10cm (4in) in
stocking (stockinette) stitch on 3mm
(UK 11, US 2/3) needles

Edge stitches:
The outermost stitch at each end of
the row is an edge stitch and worked
knit on all rows

PATTERN NOTES

This suit is worked in rows with raglan increases from the top down as far as the hips, and then worked in rounds.

On the front, the raglan stitches are worked in a pretty lace pattern following the chart on page 119, while the back raglans are worked in stocking stitch.

The suit itself is worked in stocking stitch with piping around the hips. The top part of the suit is close-fitting and fastens with buttons down the back, though these can be left out for the very small sizes. (see tip below). There is plenty of width in the hips/bottom.

Tip!

If you do not want the button fastening at the back, you can work the first 6cm (2¼in) in rows to make a back neck opening and then work in rounds. If you choose to do this, you should cast on 6 stitches fewer than the instructions say. So when you place markers, you should knit 13(14:15:16:17) sts for back 1 (before the first marker) and back 2 (before the end of round).

You can choose whether to make buttonholes or crochet a loop to close the back neck opening.

YOKE

On 2.5mm (UK 13/12, US 1/2) circular needles, cast on 86(92:98:104:108) sts and work 4 rows in garter stitch.

On the next row make a buttonhole and place markers as follows:

Next row (buttonhole row): k3,yo, k2tog, k1 (buttonband), k 10(11:12:13:14) (back 1), pm, k2 (raglan), pm, k10(11:12:13:13) (sleeve), pm, k5 (raglan), pm, k20(22:24:26:28) (front), pm, k5 (raglan), pm, k10(11:12:13:13) (sleeve), pm, k2 (raglan), k10(11:12:13:14) (back 2), k6 (buttonband).

Work one WS knit row.

Change to 3mm (UK 11, US 2/3) circular needles and work in st st, while increasing for raglan as follows:

Next row (RS inc): k6, *k to marker, m1r, sm, knit to marker, sm, m1l, k to marker, m1r, sm, work chart to marker, sm, m1l, k to marker, m1r, sm, work chart to marker, sm, m1l, k to marker, m1r, sm, knit to marker, sm, m1l, knit to end. 8 sts increased.

Next row: k6, purl to last 6 sts, k6. Repeat last 2 rows a total of 12(13:13:15:16) times, ending on a WS row, remembering to place a total of 3(4:4:5:5) buttonholes with approx. 4cm (1½in) between them. Place the buttonholes in the first 6 sts at the start of the row (on the RS) and work as follows:

Buttonhole row: k3, yo, k2tog, k1, knit to end.

After all increases there are 182(196:202:224:236) sts.

CHART

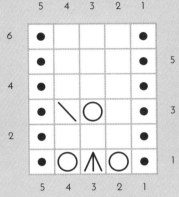

	RS: knit WS: purl
●	RS: purl WS: knit
○	yarn over
\	RS: skpo
⋀	RS: sl2, k1, psso

DIVIDE THE WORK

Next row (RS): k30(32:33:36:38), slip 34(37:38:43:45) sts for the first sleeve onto a holder, cast on 10 sts at underarm, k54(58:60:66:70), slip 34(37:38:43:45) sts for the second sleeve onto a holder, cast on 10 sts at underarm, k30(32:33:36:38). 134(142:146:158:166) sts.

The raglan stitches form part of the front and back sts, not the sleeves.

Next row (WS): k6, *purl to 1 st before cast on sts, p2tog, p8, p2tog* rep from * to * once more, p to last 6 sts, k6. 130(138:142:154:162) sts. Continue in st st until work measures 17(18:18:20:22)cm / 6¾(7:7:7¾:8¾)in) from back neck, ending on a WS row.

Now join the buttonhole bands together and then work in rounds as follows:

JOIN INTO THE ROUND

Next round: work to last 6 sts, slip them on to a spare needle, hold them behind the first 6 sts on the left needle and work the first stitch on the left needle together with the first stitch on the spare needle. Continue in this way until all 6 stitches have been knitted together. Place a marker after these sts to mark beg of round. 124(132:136:148:156) sts.

Work 2 rounds in st st.

Tip!

The piping can be worked in a contrasting colour if you want a brighter look.

PIPING

Thread a strand of a contrasting colour through all the stitches on the needle. It is important not to sew the strand into any stitches but just pull the strand through them. (If you make the piping in a different coloured yarn, there is no need to thread a contrasting colour through, this is used to mark the last round.) Work 5 rounds in stocking stitch. On the next round make the piping as follows:
On the WS, insert the right needle tip into the stitch 5 rows below the stitch on the needle, (the one immediately above the contrast strand or the first st worked in the new colour) and pick it up onto the left needle. (It is important to pick up the correct stitch, as otherwise the work will pull out of shape. If you are not sure, you can follow the stitch down on the RS, push the right needle through and thus see which stitch you should pick up.) Knit the pulled up stitch on the left needle together with the stitch next to it from the current row.

Continue in this way all the way round.

120

When all the stitches have been worked, pull out the thread (if using).

Next round: (kfb) to end. 248(264:272:296:312) sts. Work in st st until work measures 29(33:37:42:46)cm / 11½(13:14½:16½:18)in from the back neck.

Place markers as follows:

Next round: k62(66:68:74:78) (back 1), pm (this marks the side), k62(66:68:74:78) (front 1), pm (this marks the centre), k62(66:68:74:78) (front 2), pm (this marks the other side), k to end of round (back 2). On the next round decrease a total of 112(120:128:140:152) sts by working k2tog, distributed with 28(30:32:35:38) sts over each of the fronts and backs. 136(144:144:156:160) sts.

LEG BORDER

Change to 2.5mm (UK 13/12, US 1/2) DPN. Knit 1 round. Purl 1 round.

Next round (buttonhole): knit to 5 sts before the centre marker, yo, k2tog, k3, yo, sm, k2tog, k3, yo, k2tog, knit to end of round. Purl 1 round. Knit 1 round. Cast off purlwise.

SLEEVES

Transfer the 34(37:38:43:45) sleeve sts to 3mm (UK 11, US 2/3) needles and cast on 8 sts at the underarm. 42(45:46:51:53) sts.

Place a marker at the centre of the underarm to mark beg of round.

Work in rounds in st st until work measures 8(9:10:10:10)cm / 3¼(3½:4:4:4)in.

Next round (dec): k1, k2tog, k to last 3 sts, skpo, k1. 2 sts decreased.

Repeat dec round every 3(3:4:4:4)cm / 1¼:1¼:1½:1½:1½) in a total of 2(2:2:3:3) times. 38(41:42:45:47) sts.

Work in st st until sleeve measures 16(18:21:24:26)cm / 6¼(7:8¼:9½:10¼)in.

Change to 2.5mm (UK 13/12, US 1/2) needles. Knit 1 round. Purl 1 round. Knit 1 round.

Cast off loosely purlwise with 3mm (UK 11, US 2/3) needles. Work a second sleeve in the same way.

FINISHING

Sew together at underarms, darn in all the ends and sew on buttons.

NORDIC AUTUMN SWEATER

This sweater is one of my most popular patterns. The simple triangle pattern, consisting entirely of plain and purl stitches, produces a nice texture and has become a favourite with many people.

The overall pattern gives the sweater a masculine look, but it can certainly be worn by both sexes. I particularly like it in neutral colours that give it a rustic look. It is intended for autumn and cold rainy days, and the original yarn, Sterk from Du Store Alpakka, is lovely and warm and soft as well as hardwearing.

The sweater may look complicated because of the overall pattern, but it is actually quite simple to knit and even beginners could tackle it.

Sizes:
3 mths(6 mths:12 mths:18–24 mths:
3–4 yrs:5–6 yrs:7–8 yrs)

Measurements:
Chest:
44.5(50:54.5:58:64:70.5:73)cm /
17½(19¾:21½:22¾:25¼:27¾:28¾)in
Length:
28(30:32:36.5:37.5:43.5:49.5)cm /
11(11¾:12½:14½:14¾:17¼:19½)in
(from the shoulder down)

Yarn:
3(3:4:4:6:7:8) balls of Du Store
Alpakka Sterk (DK/8-ply/light
worsted); 50g/1¾oz/137m/150yd

Shown in Lys Grå Melert (light grey
melange) (841)

Suggested needles:
3mm (UK 11, US 2/3) and 3.5mm
(UK 9/10, US 4) circular needles,
40–60cm (16–24in) long;
3mm (UK 11, US 2/3) and 3.5mm
(UK 9/10, US 4) DPN

Tension (gauge):
25 sts and 35 rows to 10cm (4in)
in pattern on 3.5mm (UK 9/10,
US 4) needles

PATTERN NOTES

This sweater is worked in rounds from the bottom up. The yoke is shaped with raglan decreases. The sweater is worked in a triangle pattern with ribbed borders. It can be made with a low or high neck. The triangle pattern is shown in chart A on page 125. The raglan decreases are shown in chart B on page 127.

SLEEVES

On 3mm (UK 11, US 2/3) needles cast on 36(36:40:44:44:48:48) sts and join to work in the round. Pm to mark beg of round.
Work 3cm (1¼in) in k2, p2 rib.

Change to 3.5mm (UK 9/10, US 4) needles.
Knit 1 round, increasing 4(12:16:12:12:16:16) sts evenly spaced. It is a good idea to increase between two purl stitches. 40(48:56:56:56:64:64) sts.

On the next round work the first row of chart A and continue in pattern until work measures approx. 19(19:19:23.5:28:32.5:32.5)cm / 7½(7½:7½:9¼:11:12¾:12¾)in or desired length, ending on a row 8 of the chart.

Next round: cast (bind) off 8 sts, work chart A to end. 32(40:48:48:48:56:56) sts.
Set the remaining sts aside.
Make a second sleeve in the same way.

BODY

On 3mm (UK 11, US 2/3) needles cast on 112(128:136:144:160:176:184) sts and join to work in the round. Pm to mark beg of round.
Work 4cm (1½in) in k2, p2 rib.

Change to 3.5mm (UK 9/10, US 4) needles.

Begin pattern from chart A and continue until work measures approx. 20(20:20:24.5:24.5: 29:33.5)cm / 7¾(7¾:7¾:9½:9½: 11½:13¼)in, ending on a row 8 of the chart.

Next round (round 9): patt 20(24:32:32:32:40:40) sts, pm (start of raglan), k4, cast (bind) off 8 sts, k4, pm (end of raglan), patt 40(48:48:56:64:72:72) sts, pm (start of raglan), k4, cast (bind) off 8 sts, k4, pm (end of raglan), patt last 20(24:24:24:32:32:40) sts. 96(112:120:128:144:160:168) sts. The 4 raglan stitches will be worked in st st from here on.

YOKE

On the next round (row 10 of the chart) work the sleeves into the body as follows:

Patt to marker, sm, k4, pm (end of raglan), work the sleeve stitches on to the needle in pattern (continuing from where repeat finished), pm (start of raglan), k4 (raglan sts), continue in pattern to next marker, sm, k4, pm (end

of raglan), work sts of the second sleeve on to the needle in pattern (continuing from where repeat finished), pm (start of raglan), k4 (raglan sts), pattern to end of round.
160(192:216:224:240:272:280) sts.

Continue in chart pattern rows 11–16 of the pattern repeat as before, working all the raglan sts in st st.

Work chart row 1 once more.

RAGLAN

Next round: continuing in pattern as set, *patt to 2 sts before marker, skp0, sm, k4, sm, k2tog*, rep from * to * 3 more times, patt to end of round. 8 sts decreased.
Work 1 round without shaping.

Repeat last 2 rounds a total of 10(14:17:17:19:22:23) times, ending on a decrease round.
80(80:80:88:88:96:96) sts.

Low neck edge:
Change to 3mm (UK 11, US 2/3) needles and continue in k2, p2 rib for 2cm (¾in).

High neck:
Change to 3mm (UK 11, US 2/3) needles and continue in k2, p2 rib for 8(10:12:14:14:16:16)cm / 3¼(4:4¾:5½:5½:6¼:6¼)in.

Cast (bind) off in rib.

FINISHING
Darn in all the ends, sew the underarm seams and wash according to yarn instructions.

CHART A

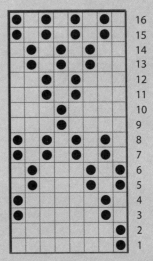

Repeat = 4.5cm (1¾in) in height

☐ RS: knit
WS: purl

⬛ RS: purl
WS: knit

☐ pattern repeat

CHART B

After raglan

Before raglan

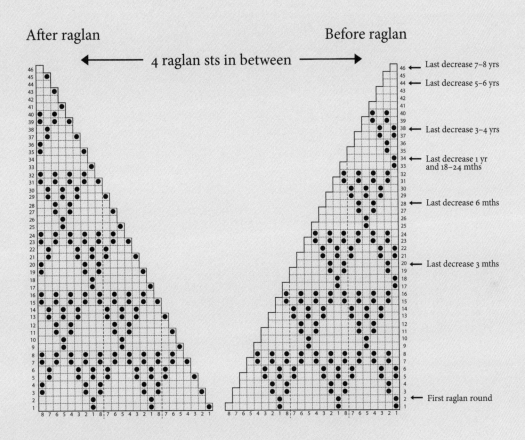

← 4 raglan sts in between →

← Last decrease 7–8 yrs
← Last decrease 5–6 yrs

← Last decrease 3–4 yrs

← Last decrease 1 yr
and 18–24 mths

← Last decrease 6 mths

← Last decrease 3 mths

← First raglan round

THOR

Nothing is as lovely as a classic ribbed sweater. The stretchy rib grows with the child, so it will fit for a long time. It is comfortable to wear, because it never feels tight, even though it fits closely. This makes it perfect for everyday life as a child. This is my version of the classic ribbed sweater.

Thor has a nice smock pattern on the front to liven it up a bit and give it a rustic look. It has a medium-height neck for protection against cool weather and emphasizes the shoulders and chest. The sweater is called Thor, after the Norse god of thunder, because it looks strong and the smock pattern resembles lightning, breaking up an otherwise conservative rib pattern.

This sweater pattern is suitable for girls as well as for boys.

Sizes:
6 mths(1 yr:2 yrs:4 yrs:6 yrs)

Measurements:
Chest:
48(51:54:63:68)cm /
19(20:21¼:24¾:26¾)in
Length:
29(32:35:38:43)cm /
11½(12½:13¾:15:17)in
(measured from the
shoulder down)

Yarn:
3(3:4:4:5) balls of Du Store Alpakka
Sterk (DK/8-ply/light worsted);
50g/1¾oz/137m/150yd
Shown in Natur (natural) (806)

Suggested needles:
3mm (UK 11, US 2/3) and 3.5mm
(UK 9/10, US 4) circular needles,
40–60cm (16–24in) long;
3mm (UK 11, US 2/3) and 3.5mm
(UK 9/10, US 4) DPN

Tension (gauge):
28 sts and 34 rows to 10cm (4in) in
k2, p2 rib, (slightly stretched), on
3.5mm (UK 9/10, US 4) needles

Special abbreviations:
Smock6: insert right needle into
space between sts 6 and 7 on left
needle, wrap yarn around needle as
if to knit and pull through to front
of work, slip the loop made onto the
left needle and knit together with the
next knit st, k1, p2, k2.

PATTERN NOTES

The sweater is worked in rounds from the top down. The yoke is shaped with raglan increases. The entire sweater is worked in rib, but with a smock pattern along the raglan on the front on every eighth round.

NECK

On 3.5mm (UK 9/10, US 4) needles, cast on 80(80:80:88:88) sts and join to work in the round. Pm to mark beg of round.

Next round: p1, (k2, p2) to last 3 sts, k2, p1.
Repeat last round until work measures 3(3:4:4:5)cm / 1¼(1¼:1½:1½:2)in.

Place markers as follows:
Next round: rib 13(13:13:17:17) sts (back 1), pm, k2 (raglan), pm, rib 10(10:10:6:6) (sleeve), pm, k2 (raglan), pm, rib 26(26:26:34:34) sts (front), pm, k2 (raglan), pm, rib 10(10:10:6:6) sts (sleeve), pm, k2 (raglan), rib 13(13:13:17:17) sts (back 2).

RAGLAN

Round 1 (inc): *patt to marker, m1r, sm, k2, sm, m1l*, rep from * to * 3 more times, pattern to end. 8 sts increased.
Round 2: patt to end.
Round 3: rep inc round.
Round 4 (smock): patt to marker, sm, k2, sm, patt to marker, sm, k2, sm, *smock6, p2* rep from * to * to last 6 sts of front, smock6, sm, patt to end.

Last round sets placement for smock pattern. Note that the pattern will naturally become staggered as increases are made.

Work the smock row across the front sts every round 4 until it has been worked 4(4:5:5:6) times, at the same time increasing every alt round until a total of 16(16:20:20:24) inc rounds have been worked, ending on a non-inc round. 208(208:240:248:280) sts.

DIVIDE FOR SLEEVES
Next round: patt 31(31:35:39:43) sts to first sleeve, transfer 42(42:50:46:54) sts to scrap yarn for the sleeve, cast on 6(10:6:10:10) sts at underarm, pattern 62(62:70:78:86) sts, transfer 42(42:50:46:54) sts to scrap yarn for the second sleeve, cast on 6(10:6:10:10) sts at underarm, pattern to end of round. Note the raglan stitches are now part of the back and the front. 136(144:152:176:192) sts.

BODY

Continue in rib, bringing new sts into pattern until work measures 27(30:33:36:41)cm / 10¾(11¾:13:14¼:16¼)in from the shoulder down or 2cm (¾in) before the desired length.

Change to 3mm (UK 11, US 2/3) needles.

Work a further 2cm (¾in) in rib.

Cast (bind) off in rib with 3.5mm
(UK 9/10, US 4) needles.

SLEEVES

Transfer the 42(42:50:46:54)
sts of the sleeve to 3.5mm
(UK 9/10, US 4) DPN and cast
on 6(10:6:10:10) sts at underarm.
48(52:56:56:64) sts. Place a marker
at the centre of the underarm
between two knit stitches to mark
the start of the round.

Work in k2, p2 rib until
work measures 2(2:3:3:3)cm /
¼(¾:1½:1½:1½)in.

Next round (dec): patt2tog, patt to
2 sts before the marker, patt2tog.

Repeat decrease round a total of
6(8:8:8:12) times, with
2(2:3:3:3)cm / ¼(¾:1½:1½:1½)
in between decrease rows.
36(36:40:40:40) sts.

Continue without shaping until
sleeve measures 19(22:26:30:34)cm
/ 7½(8¾:10¾:11¾:13½)in from the
armhole and cast (bind) off in rib.

FINISHING

Sew underarm seams and darn in
all the ends.

SHELTERED

Sheltered means being covered and protected both against inclement weather and against harm, and that is exactly what I had in mind when I designed this baby blanket.

In Denmark it is a part of our culture to go for long walks with our little ones in a pushchair. It is lovely to have a blanket that can be spread over bare legs in summer and provide extra warmth in winter. The blanket is perfect for wrapping round your newborn baby and providing a sense of security. It follows the child around and can be used as a play rug or for cuddling up on the sofa when the child gets older.

The blanket is easy to knit, a lovely project that will create many happy memories in the future.

Measurements:
Approx. 75 x 90cm (27½ x 35½in) after blocking

Yarn:
8 balls of Dale of Norway/Dalegarn Cotinga (aran/10-ply/worsted); 50g/1¾oz/80m/88yd
Shown in Ubleget Hvid (unbleached white) (0020) pages 132 and 134, Syren (lilac) (5302) and Mosegrøn (moss green) (8231) page 134

Suggested needles:
4.5mm (UK 7, US 7) circular needle, 60cm (24in) long

Tension (gauge):
18 sts and 26 rows to 10cm (4in) in pattern on 4.5mm (UK 7, US 7) needles

Edge stitches:
The 5 outermost stitches are edge stitches and should be worked knit on all rows

Tip:

You can make the blanket bigger by adding a couple of extra pattern repeats and making it longer. However, do not forget that this will require extra yarn.

PATTERN NOTES

The baby blanket is worked in rows in a lovely lacy pattern with garter stitch borders. The pattern is worked from the chart on page 135.

BLANKET

On 4.5mm (UK 7, US 7) needles cast on 132 sts and work 12 rows in garter stitch (knit on all rows).

Begin lace pattern
Next row (RS): k5 (edge sts), work from chart to last 5 sts, k5 (edge sts).
Continuing as set, work the chart between the 5 edge sts either side which should be worked in garter stitch. Read the chart from right to left on right side rows and left to right on wrong side rows.

On the wrong side work purl over purl and knit over knit. Repeat the first 14 stitches (shown in the red box) 8 times, then work the last 10 stitches of the chart (stitches 15–24 of the chart).

Work rows 1–22 of chart 9 times in total.

Work 11 rows in garter stitch and cast (bind) off all stitches knitwise on next row (WS).

FINISHING

Darn in all the ends on the wrong side of the work.
Wash the blanket according to the instructions on the ball band, spread it out so that the lace pattern opens up and dry flat.

CHART

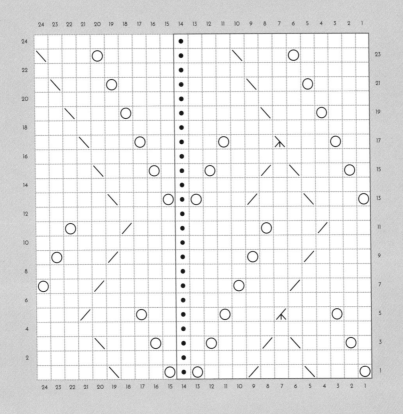

	RS: knit WS: purl	/	k2tog
•	RS: purl WS: knit	⋏	k3tog
○	yarn over	⋌	sl1, k2tog, psso
\	sl1, k1, psso		pattern repeat

FANCY COLLAR

A little collar can smarten up any outfit. Add it to a pretty dress for a special occasion or use it to liven up an everyday combination of trousers and a sweater. The pattern for the Fancy Collar came about when I was knitting various samples for Charming and trying out different ways of using beads. My four-year-old daughter thought it was amazingly pretty and exciting and was very eager to decorate herself with the yarn that had beads threaded on it. Of course that would not do, so I had to set to work and come up with something to adorn her with, and it turned out to be this pretty beaded collar.

Both my kids love putting on pretty things and dressing up, just like many other children. The Fancy Collar gives children a chance to choose beads and their favourite colour of yarn and it is quick to knit, so it does not take long to make a few different collars for their wardrobe.

Measurements:
One size; the inside neck measurement is approx. 33cm (13in)

Yarn:
1 ball of CaMaRose Yaku 4/16 (4-ply/fingering); 50g/1¾oz/200m/219yd
Shown in Råhvid (off white) (1000)

Suggested needles:
3mm (UK 11, US 2/3) and 2.5mm (UK 13/12, US 1/2) needles

Beads:
Approx. 295, 3.8–4.5mm (⅛–³⁄₁₆in) diameter

Other materials:
Thin nylon thread or a beading needle

Tension (gauge):
27 sts to 10cm (4in) in st st on 3mm (UK 11, US 2/3) needles

Tip:

Add a band of lace at the neck to give the collar an even sweeter look.

PATTERN NOTES

The collar is worked in stocking (stockinette) stitch, with beads in staggered rows on every other stitch. The two sides of the collar are worked separately and sewn together at the front afterwards. The outermost stitches at each end of the row are edge stitches and should be worked knitwise on all rows. The wrong side rows are purled and are not included in the instructions below.

Thread the beads on to the yarn using a beading needle or a thin nylon thread.

The collar is shaped using German short rows (see Techniques, page 11).

Bead on right side:
Bring the yarn to the front of the work, pull the bead down and slip one stitch purlwise.
Stretch the yarn to the back of the work and knit the next stitch. The bead is now sitting in front of the slipped stitch.

TO START

Thread approx 295 beads on to the yarn before beginning each side. Complete each side separately as follows:

With 2.5mm (UK 13/12, US 1/2) needles cast on 44 sts.
Knit 2 rows.
Change to 3mm (UK 11, US 2/3) needles and continue with either the left or the right piece.

LEFT PIECE

Row 1 (RS): k1 (bead 1, k1) to last st, k1. 44 sts, 21 beads.
Row 2 and all WS rows to row 22: k1, purl to last st, k1.
Row 3: k2, (bead 1, k1) to end of row. 44 sts, 21 beads.
Row 5: k1, (bead 1, k1) to last 3 sts, bead 1, k2tog. 43 sts, 21 beads.
Row 7: k2, (bead 1, k1) 3 times, bead 1, kfb, m1l, *(bead 1, k1) twice, bead 1, kfb, m1l*, rep from * to * 3 more times, (bead 1, k1) to last 3 sts, bead 1, k2tog. 52 sts, 20 beads.
Row 9: k1, (bead 1, k1) to last 3 sts, bead 1, k2tog. 51 sts, 25 beads.
Row 11: k2, (bead 1, k1) to last 3 sts, bead 1, k2tog. 50 sts, 24 beads.
Row 13: k1, (bead 1, k1) to last 3 sts, bead 1, k2tog. 49 sts, 24 beads.
Row 15: k2, (bead 1, k1) 6 times, bead 1, kfb, m1l, (bead 1, k1) 7 times, bead 1, kfb, m1l, (bead 1, k1) to last 3 sts, bead 1, k2tog. 52 sts, 23 beads.
Row 17: k1, (bead 1, k1) to last 3 sts, bead 1, k2tog. 51 sts, 25 beads.
Row 19: skpo, (bead 1, k1) to last 3 sts, bead 1, k2tog. 49 sts, 24 beads.
Row 21: skpo, (bead 1, k1) * to last 3 sts, bead 1, k2tog. 47 sts, 23 beads.
Row 23: skpo, (bead 1, k1) to last 7 sts, turn the work (German short rows), purl all sts. 46 sts, 19 beads.
Row 24: p2, p1 in front loop without taking the stitch off the needle, then p1 in back loop, purl to end of row. 47 sts.

Row 25: skpo, (bead 1, k1) to turning st, pull the bead forward and work double stitch tog, (bead 1, k1) to last 3 sts, bead 1, k2tog. 46 sts, 22 beads.

Row 26 (WS): cast (bind) off knitwise.

RIGHT PIECE

Row 1 (RS): k2 (bead 1, k1) to end of row. 44 sts, 21 beads.

Row 2 and all WS rows to row 22: k1, purl to last st, k1.

Row 3: k1, (bead 1, k1) to last st, k1. 44 sts, 21 beads.

Row 5: skpo (bead 1, k1) to end of row. 43 sts, 21 beads.

Row 7: skpo, (bead 1, k1) twice, bead 1, kfb, m1l, *(bead 1, k1) twice, bead 1, kfb, m1l*, rep from * to * 3 more times, (bead 1, k1) to last st, k1. 52 sts, 20 beads.

Row 9: skpo, (bead 1, k1) to end of row. 51 sts, 25 beads.

Row 11: skpo, (bead 1, k1) to last st, k1. 50 sts, 24 beads.

Row 13: skpo, (bead 1, k1) to end of row. 49 sts, 24 beads.

Row 15: skpo (bead 1, k1) 8 times, bead 1, kfb, m1l, (bead 1, k1) 7 times, bead 1, kfb, m1l, (bead 1, k1) to last st, k1. 52 sts, 23 beads.

Row 17: skpo (bead 1, k1) to end of row. 51 sts 25 beads.

Row 19: skpo, (bead 1, k1) to last 3 sts, bead 1, k2tog. 49 sts, 24 beads.

Row 21: skpo, (bead 1, k1) to last 3 sts, bead 1, k2tog. 47 sts, 23 beads.

Rows 22 and 23 (WS): purl to last 7 sts, turn the work (German short rows), work (bead 1, k1) to last 3 sts, bead 1, k2tog. 46 sts, 20 beads.

Row 24 (WS): purl to 1 st before turning stitch, p1 in front loop without taking the stitch off the needle, then p1 in back loop. Purl the two parts of the turning stitch together and continue in purl to end of row. 47 sts.

Row 25: skpo, (bead 1, k1) to last 3 sts, bead 1, k2tog. 45 sts, 22 beads.

Row 26: (WS): k2tog, cast (bind) off knitwise.

FINISHING

Darn in all the ends. Sew a ribbon to the end of each of the two pieces, for tying together at the back of the neck. Sew the two pieces together at the front with a couple of stitches at the top.

MATERIALS

YARNS

Below each yarn used in the book are some suggested substitutes which may be more widely available. Please remember to swatch to check tension (gauge) first and go up or down a needle size if necessary!

The yarns in Group 1 can be substituted for one another. However, you should pay attention to the yardage so you do not run out of yarn. Sandnes Alpakka Silke can also be included in this category, but in this case, it is important to be aware that it is a silk yarn and will therefore have a different effect from the others.

GROUP 1:

**CAMAROSE YAKU 4/16
(4-PLY/FINGERING)**
100% superwash pure new wool,
50g/1¾oz/200m/219yd
Tension (gauge): 28 sts to 10cm (4in)
over st st on 2.5–3mm
(UK 13/12–11, US 1/2–2/3) needles

Suggested substitutes:
**Lang Yarns Merino 200
Bébé**   100% merino wool,
50g/1¾oz/203m/222yd
Tension (gauge): 28 sts and 32 rows to
10cm (4in) over st st on 2.5–3mm
(UK 13/12–11, US 1/2–2/3) needles

For each ball of CaMaRose Yaku 4/16
you will need 1 ball of this.

Fyberspates Vivacious 4-ply   100%
merino wool, 100g/3½oz/365m/399yd
Tension (gauge): 26 sts and 30 rows
to 10cm (4in) over st st on 2.5–3mm
(UK 13/12–11, US 1/2–2/3) needles

For each ball of CaMaRose Yaku 4/16
you will need 0.55 skeins of this.

McIntosh BFL 4-ply   100% wool,
100g/3½oz/400m/437yd
Tension (gauge): 28 sts and 36 rows
to 10cm (4in) over st st on 2.5–3mm
(UK 13/12–11, US 1/2–2/3) needles

For each ball of CaMaRose Yaku 4/16
you will need 0.5 skeins of this.

FILCOLANA: ARWETTA CLASSIC (4-PLY/ FINGERING)
80% superwash merino wool, 20% nylon, 50g/1¾oz/210m/230yd
Tension (gauge): 28–32 sts to 10cm (4in) over st st on 2.5–3mm (UK 13/12–11, US 1/2–2/3) needles

Suggested substitutes:
Knitpicks Stroll 75% superwash merino wool, 25% nylon, 50g/1¾oz/211m/231yd
Tension (gauge): 28–32 sts to 10cm (4in) over st st on 2.25–3.25mm (UK 13–10, US 1–3) needles

For each ball of Filcolana Arwetta Classic you will need 1 skein of this.

Coop Knits Socks Yeah!
75% superwash merino wool, 25% nylon, 50g/1¾oz/212m/232yd
Tension (gauge): 36 sts and 50 rows to 10cm (4in) over st st on 2.25–2.75mm (UK 13–12, US 1–2) needles

For each ball of Filcolana Arwetta Classic you will need 1 skein of this.

Cascade Yarns Heritage
75% superwash merino wool, 25% nylon, 100g/3½oz/400m/437yd
Tension (gauge): 28–32 sts to 10cm (4in) over st st on 2.25–3.25mm (UK 13–10, US 1–3) needles

For each ball of Filcolana Arwetta Classic you will need 0.53 skeins of this.

SANDNES TYNN MERINOULL (4-PLY/ FINGERING)
100% superwash merino wool, 50g/1¾oz/175m/191yd
Tension (gauge): 27 sts to 10cm (4in) over st st on 3mm (UK 11, US 2/3) needles

Suggested substitutes:
Schachenmayr Original: Merino Extrafine 170 100% merino wool, 50g/1¾oz/170m/186yd
Tension (gauge): 28 sts and 36 rows to 10cm (4in) over st st on 3mm (UK 11, US 2/3) needles

For each ball of Sandnes Tynn Merinoull you will need 1.03 balls of this.

Debbie Bliss Rialto 4-ply
100% merino wool, 50g/1¾oz/181m/198yd
Tension (gauge): 28 sts and 36 rows to 10cm (4in) over st st on 3.25mm (UK 10, US 3) needles

For each ball of Sandnes Tynn Merinoull you will need 1 ball of this.

DROPS Baby Merino 100% wool, 50g/1¾oz/175m/191yd
Tension (gauge): 24 sts and 32 rows to 10cm (4in) over st st on 3mm (UK 11, US 2/3) needles

For each ball of Sandnes Tynn Merinoull you will need 1 ball of this.

Continued overleaf.

Lang Yarns Merino 150 100% Merino Wool, 50g/1¾oz/150m/164yd Tension (gauge): 27 sts and 37 rows to 10cm (4in) over st st on 3–3.5mm (UK 11–10/9, US 2/3–4) needles

For each ball of Sandnes Tynn Merinoull you will need 1.17 balls of this.

DU STORE ALPAKKA MINI STERK (4-PLY/ FINGERING) 40% alpaca, 40% merino wool, 20% nylon, 50g/1¾oz/166m/181yd Tension (gauge): 27 sts to 10cm (4in) over st st on 3mm (UK 11, US 2/3) needles

Suggested substitutes:
Madeline Tosh Twist Light 100% superwash merino wool, 100g/3½oz/384m/420yd Tension (gauge): 26–30 sts to 10cm (4in) over st st on 2.25–2.75mm (UK 13–12, US 1–2) needles

For each ball of Du Store Alpakka Mini Sterk you will need 0.43 balls of this.

Knitpicks Hawthorn Fingering 80% Highland superwash wool, 20% nylon, 100g/3½oz/326m/356yd Tension (gauge): 26–30 sts to 10cm (4in) over st st on 2.25–3.5mm (UK 13–10/9, US 1–4) needles

For each ball of Du Store Alpakka Mini Sterk you will need 0.51 balls of this.

FILCOLANA ANINA (4-PLY/FINGERING) 100% superwash treated pure new wool, 50g/1¾oz/210m/230yd Tension (gauge): 26–28 sts to 10cm (4in) over st st on 3–3.5mm (UK 11–9/10, US 2/3–4) needles

Suggested substitutes:
Cascade Yarns 220 Superwash Fingering 100% merino wool, 100g/3½oz/200m/219yd Tension (gauge): 28 sts and 32 rows to 10cm (4in) over st st on 2.25–3.25mm (UK 13–10, US 1–3) needles

For each ball of Filcolana Anina you will need 1.05 balls of this.

Cascade Yarns Heritage Silk 85% merino wool, 15% silk, 100g/3½oz/400m/437yd Tension (gauge): 28 sts and 32 rows to 10cm (4in) over st st on 2.25–3.25mm (UK 13–10, US 1–3) needles

For each ball of Filcolana Anina you will need 0.53 balls of this.

Knitpicks: Capretta Superwash 80% fine superwash merino, 10% cashmere, 10% nylon, 50g/1¾oz/210m/230yd Tension (gauge): 28 sts and 32 rows to 10cm (4in) over st st on 2.25–3.25mm (UK 13–10, US 1–3) needles

For each ball of Filcolana Anina you will need 1 ball of this.

OTHER YARNS

SANDNES ALPAKKA SILKE (4-PLY/FINGERING)
70% baby alpaca, 30% mulberry silk, 50g/1¾oz/200m/218½yd
Tension (gauge): 27 sts to 10cm (4in) over st st on 3mm (UK 11, US 2/3) needles

Suggested substitute:
Holst Garn Haya 70% baby alpaca, 20% mulberry silk, 10% yak, 50g/1¾oz/183m/200yd
Tension (gauge): 28 sts to 10cm (4in) over st st on 3–3.5mm (UK 11–10/9, US 2/3–4) needles

For each ball of Sandnes Alpakka Silke you will need 1.09 balls of this.

SANDNES MERINOULL (DK/8-PLY/LIGHT WORSTED)
100% superwash merino wool, 50g/1¾oz/105m/115yd
Tension (gauge): 22 sts to 10cm (4in) over st st on 4mm (UK 8, US 6) needles

Suggested substitutes:
Viking of Norway Merino 100% merino wool, 50g/1¾oz/105m/115yd
Tension (gauge): 22 sts to 10cm (4in) over st st on 4mm (UK 8, US 6) needles.

For each ball of Sandnes Merinoull you will need 1 ball of this.

Schachenmayr Original Merino Extrafine 120 100% merino wool, 50g/1¾oz/120m/131½yd
Tension (gauge): 22 sts and 30 rows to 10cm (4in) over st st on 3–4mm (UK 11–8, US 2/3–6) needles

For each ball of Sandnes Merinoull you will need 0.88 balls of this.

Lang Yarns Merino 120
100% merino wool, 50g/1¾oz/120m/131½yd
Tension (gauge): 22 sts and 32 rows to 10cm (4in) over st st on 3.5–4.5mm (UK 10/9–7, US 4–7) needles

For each ball of Sandnes Merinoull you will need 0.88 balls of this.

DALE OF NORWAY/DALEGARN COTINGA (ARAN/10-PLY/WORSTED)
70% merino wool, 30% alpaca, 50g/1¾oz/80m/88yd
Tension (gauge): 18 sts to 10cm (4in) over st st on 4.5–5mm (UK 7–5, US 7–8) needles

Suggested substitute:
West Yorkshire Spinners The Croft Shetland Aran
100g/3oz/166m/182yd
Tension (gauge): 18 sts and 24 rows to 10cm (4in) over st st on 5mm (UK 6, US 8) needles

For each ball of Dale of Norway/Dalegarn Cotinga you will need 0.48 balls of this.

Continued overleaf.

**DU STORE ALPAKKA
STERK (DK/8-PLY/LIGHT
WORSTED)** 40% alpaca,
40% merino wool, 20% nylon.
50g/1¾oz/137m/150yd
Tension (gauge): 22 sts to 10cm
(4in) over st st on 3.5mm (UK 9/10,
US 4) needles

Suggested substitute:
Valley Yarns Northfield
70% merino wool, 20% alpaca,
10% silk, 50g/1¾oz/113m/124yd
Tension (gauge): 22 sts to 10cm
(4in) over st st on 4mm (UK 8,
US 6) needles

For each ball of Du Store Alpakka
Sterk you will need 0.83 balls of this.

OTHER MATERIALS

Buttons
House of Yarn, Søstrene Grene,
private button collection

Beads
Panduro Hobby, Rocailles beads,
3.8–4.5mm (⅛–³⁄₁₆in) diameter

Beading needle
Panduro Hobby